Treasures

Grade 3

Grammar
AND
Writing
Handbook

Macmillan/McGraw-Hill

A

The *McGraw·Hill* Companies

Macmillan McGraw-Hill

Published by Macmillan/McGraw-Hill, of McGraw-Hill Education, a division of The McGraw-Hill Companies, Inc., Two Penn Plaza, New York, New York 10121.

Printed in the United States of America

1 2 3 4 5 6 7 8 9 079 11 10 09 08 07

Writing

Contents

Contents

Writing

Writing

Grammar

Contents

Contents

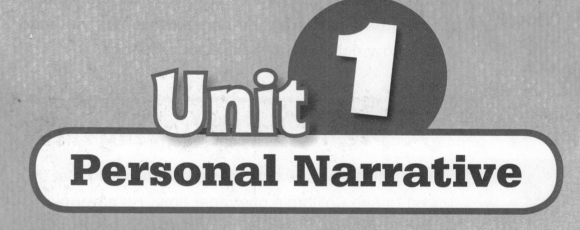

Unit **1**
Personal Narrative

Personal Narrative

A personal narrative is a true story that you tell about yourself. When you write a personal narrative, you tell about something that happened to you and how you felt about it.

Learning from Writers

Read the following examples of personal narrative. What stories do the writers tell? Why do you think they wanted to share their experiences? As you read, notice how each author tells about feelings.

THINK AND WRITE

Purpose

Why do you think people write personal narratives? Explain what you think in your journal. Also tell why people like to read them.

A Man of Two Countries

The last time I saw him, my grandfather said that he longed to see California one more time. He never did.

And when I was nearly grown, I left home and went to see California for myself.

After a time, I came to love the land my grandfather had loved, and I stayed on and on until I had a daughter of my own.

But I also miss the mountains and rivers of my childhood. I miss my old friends. So I return now and then, when I can not still the longing in my heart.

The funny thing is, the moment I am in one country, I am homesick for the other.

— Allen Say, from *Grandfather's Journey*

The Canoe Trip That Never Happened

Last summer, my mom and my aunt suggested we go canoeing on the Green River. I was excited! Before we left, we bought a new tent and life jackets. We studied maps and planned where we should camp each night.

Early one morning, we packed up the car and drove to the Green River. Surprise! The river was brown and full of trash. There had been so much rain, it was flooding. Our careful plans were ruined.

We stayed in motels and visited museums. It was okay, but not as much fun as canoeing. I hope we can try again next year.

— Maryann Kopek

PRACTICE AND APPLY

Thinking Like a Reader

1. Name three events in Allen Say's narrative in the order they happened.

2. How did Maryann Kopek feel before and after the canoe trip?

Thinking Like a Writer

3. How did the author let you know the order of events in "A Man of Two Countries"?

4. What words did Maryann Kopek use to show how she felt?

5. **Reading Across Texts** Compare the beginning paragraphs of the two personal narratives. Write about how they are alike and different.

Features of Personal Narrative

DEFINITIONS AND FEATURES

A personal narrative is writing that tells a true story about your own life. A good personal narrative:

▶ Tells a story from the writer's **personal experience** using words like *I, my,* and *me.*

▶ Expresses the writer's **feelings**.

▶ Has an **interesting beginning, middle,** and **ending**.

▶ Uses **time-order words** to share events in the order they happened.

▶ A Personal Experience

Reread "A Man of Two Countries" on page 8. Who is the story about?

> So I return now and then, when I can not still the longing in my heart.

The words *I* and *my* let you know that the author is telling about an experience in his own life.

▶ The Writer's Feelings

What words does the author use to tell you about his feelings?

> But I also miss the mountains and rivers of my childhood. I miss my old friends.

When the author says, "I miss my old friends," you can tell he is feeling sad.

► An Interesting Beginning, Middle, and Ending

How does Allen Say catch your attention with this beginning?

> The last time I saw him, my grandfather said that he longed to see California one more time.

This beginning may make you wonder why his grandfather's wish was important to the author.

Why is the following sentence a good ending?

> The funny thing is, the moment I am in one country, I am homesick for the other.

► Time-Order Words

To help your reader clearly understand what happened, use time-order words and phrases such as *at first, then, last week,* and *finally.*

> After a time, I came to love the land my grandfather had loved . . .

What time-order phrase did the author use?

PRACTICE AND APPLY

Create a Features Chart

1. List the features of a good personal narrative.

2. Reread "The Canoe Trip That Never Happened" by Maryann Kopek on page 9.

3. Write one example of each feature in Maryann's writing.

4. Write what you liked about Maryann's personal narrative.

Features	Examples

Writing PROCESS

Prewrite

A personal narrative is a true story about yourself. Writing a personal narrative gives you a chance to tell about your own life.

Purpose and Audience

The purpose for writing a personal narrative is to share how you feel about an experience in your life. It is also to entertain your readers, or audience.

Before you begin to write, think about your audience. Who will be reading your story? How can you help your readers get to know you?

Choose a Topic

Begin by **brainstorming** a list of people who are special to you. Choose one person to write about. Then **explore ideas** by listing what you remember about being with this person.

THINK AND WRITE

Audience

How will you help your readers know how you feel about a special person? Write your answer.

I explored my ideas by making a list.

Aunt Jane

Aunt Jane is fun
Lets me try new things
Taught me how to swim
Let me feed baby Alex
Alex spit out the food

Organize • Clustering

Your narrative will have two main parts. First, you will tell about a special person. Then you will tell about something that happened when you were with that person. To plan your narrative, you can use a cluster map. How did this writer organize the ideas from his list?

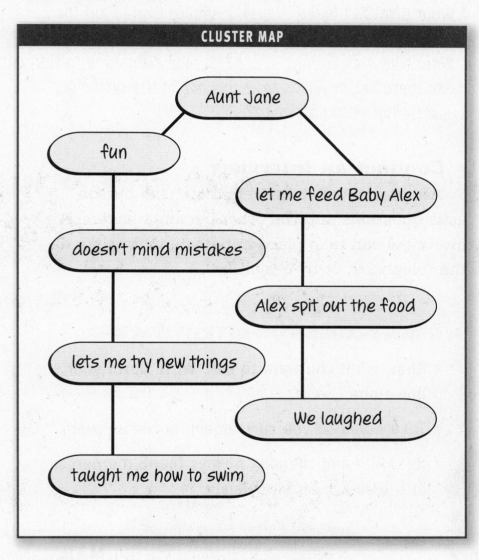

CLUSTER MAP

Aunt Jane

fun

doesn't mind mistakes

let me feed Baby Alex

Alex spit out the food

lets me try new things

We laughed

taught me how to swim

Checklist ✓
Prewriting

■ **Have you thought about your purpose and audience?**

■ **Have you chosen one person and event to tell about?**

■ **Have you made a list of ideas about the person and the experience?**

■ **Are your ideas organized in a cluster map?**

■ **Do you need to do any research?**

PRACTICE AND APPLY

Plan Your Own Personal Narrative

1. Think about your purpose and audience.

2. Choose a topic.

3. Brainstorm ideas about your topic.

4. Organize your ideas.

Prewrite • Research and Inquiry

► Writer's Resources

You may need to get more information for your personal narrative. Make a list of questions. Then decide where you can find the answers.

What Else Do I Need to Know?	Where Can I Find the Information?
What was Alex eating?	E-mail Aunt Jane to find out.
Are there better words to describe what happened?	Look in the dictionary.

► Conduct an Interview

An interview is a conversation. One person asks questions and the other person answers. An interview can take place in person, in writing, on the telephone, or by e-mail.

STRATEGIES FOR INTERVIEWING

- Know what you want to ask. Write down your questions.

- Take notes so you can remember the answers.

- Be polite and friendly. Always thank the person at the end of an interview.

MAILMAX

MAILMAX

new   read   file   print   save   delete

Aunt Jane, do you remember the first time I tried to feed Alex? What was that orange food in the jar?

Timmy, it was strained squash.

▶ Use a Dictionary

You can find the spelling and meanings of words in a dictionary. Use alphabetical order to find words. Sometimes the dictionary meaning of a word can tell you other ways to say the same thing.

▶ Use Your Research

New information gathered from your research can go into your cluster map. This writer learned two things from his research. How did he change his map?

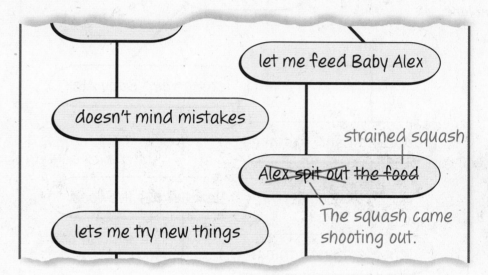

let me feed Baby Alex

doesn't mind mistakes

strained squash

~~Alex spit out the food~~

lets me try new things

The squash came shooting out.

Checklist ✔

Research and Inquiry

- ■ Did you list your questions?

- ■ Did you identify possible resources?

- ■ Did you take notes?

PRACTICE AND APPLY

Review Your Plan

1. Look at your cluster map.

2. List questions you have about your topic.

3. Identify the resources you will need to find answers.

4. Add new information you gather to your map.

Draft

Before you begin writing your personal narrative, review the cluster map you made. Think about making a paragraph for each main idea. Include details that support each main idea.

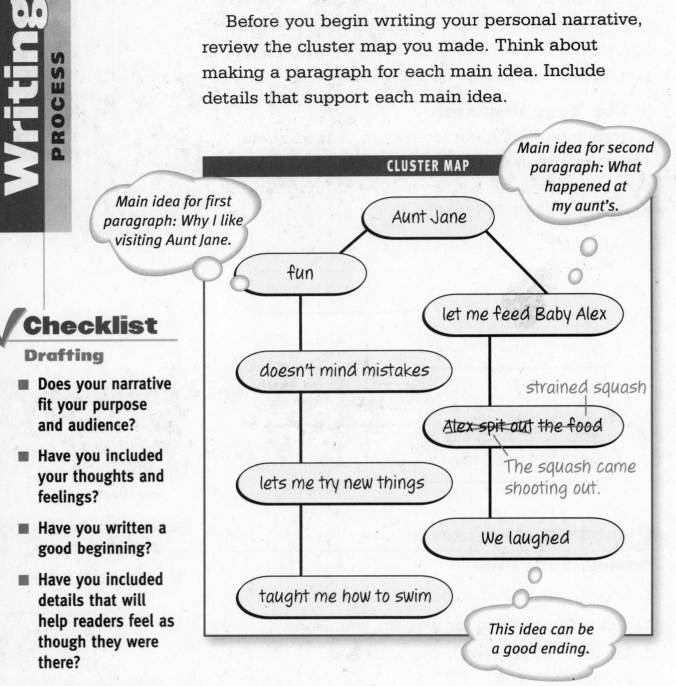

Main idea for first paragraph: Why I like visiting Aunt Jane.

Main idea for second paragraph: What happened at my aunt's.

CLUSTER MAP

Aunt Jane

fun

let me feed Baby Alex

doesn't mind mistakes

strained squash

~~Alex spit out the food~~

The squash came shooting out.

lets me try new things

We laughed

taught me how to swim

This idea can be a good ending.

Writing
PROCESS

✓ Checklist

Drafting

- Does your narrative fit your purpose and audience?

- Have you included your thoughts and feelings?

- Have you written a good beginning?

- Have you included details that will help readers feel as though they were there?

- Does your narrative have an interesting ending?

Look at how this writer used the ideas in his cluster map to write a first draft. He added details about Aunt Jane in the first paragraph. Then he told about something that happened when he was with her.

DRAFT

This is about my Aunt Jane. Keeps me busy all the time. We have a lot of fun together, even when I make mistakes. She lets me try new things. She even taught me how to swim.

One time a very funny thing happened. Baby Alex was hungry. Aunt Jane asked, "Do you want to try feeding him." So we put Alex into his high chair. We got out a jar of strained squash. I spooned some into Alex's mouth. It came shooting right back out! It got all over me. Alex made a funny face Aunt Jane and I just laughed and laughed.

Main idea of first paragraph

Supporting details tell about the writer's aunt.

Main idea of second paragraph

Supporting details tell what happened.

PRACTICE AND APPLY

Draft Your Own Personal Narrative

1. Review your prewriting cluster map.

2. Write about how you felt.

3. Tell about things in the order they happened.

TECHNOLOGY

Find out how to change line spacing on your computer. It's a good idea to double space your draft so that you have room to write in changes after you print it out.

17

Revise

Elaborate

One way to improve your writing is to elaborate. When you elaborate, you add important ideas and details that create a clear picture for the reader. When you revise your personal narrative, you may need to tell more about your feelings.

The writer added a detail that helps the reader know how he feels.

I love to visit

~~This is about~~ my Aunt Jane.

The writer added a description of where the food went to help the reader picture what happened.

my clothes. It was even in my hair.

It got all over me.

Word Choice

When you write, it is important to choose just the right words for your topic and audience.

In a personal narrative, you need to find words that will help you tell the events in the order they happened.

First,

So we put Alex into his high chair. Then We got out

a jar of strained squash.

TIME-ORDER WORDS

first
next
then
later
after
last
before
as soon as
finally
this morning
yesterday
last summer
tomorrow
a long time ago

Better Sentences

As you are revising your draft, read your sentences aloud. How do they sound? Have you used different kinds of sentences? You can change the rhythm of your writing by combining two sentences.

Use *and* to connect two related sentences.

> We got out a jar of strained squash, *and* I spooned some into Alex's mouth.

PRACTICE AND APPLY

Revise Your Own Personal Narrative

1. Add details that will make your writing clearer and more interesting.

2. Use words that help the reader know exactly how you felt.

3. Take out information that isn't necessary.

4. **Grammar** Should you combine any sentences?

TECHNOLOGY

Learn how to cut and paste on the computer so that you can easily move sentences and parts of sentences when you revise.

Revise • Peer Conferencing

Read the first draft of your personal narrative aloud to your partner. Your partner may give you some new ideas and suggestions.

How do you feel about Aunt Jane?

This detail belongs in another story.

When did this happen?

This ending makes me smile.

This is about my Aunt Jane. Keeps me busy all the time. We have a lot of fun together, even when I make mistakes. She lets me try new things. She even taught me how to swim.

One time a very funny thing happened. Baby Alex was hungry. Aunt Jane asked, "Do you want to try feeding him." So we put Alex into his high chair. We got out a jar of strained squash. I spooned some into Alex's mouth. It came shooting right back out! It got all over me. Alex made a funny face Aunt Jane and I just laughed and laughed.

Conferencing for the Reader

■ Did your partner include features of a personal narrative?
  • personal experience and feelings
  • interesting beginning, middle, and ending
  • time-order words
■ Tell your partner what is good about the piece, as well as what could be better.

Think about the comments and suggestions of your partner when you revise your personal narrative. This writer made some changes based on his partner's ideas.

REVISE

My Aunt Jane

I love to visit

~~This is about~~ my Aunt Jane. Keeps me busy all

the time. We have a lot of fun together, even when

Best of all,

I make mistakes. She lets me try new things. ~~She~~

~~even taught me how to swim.~~

When I visited Aunt Jane last summer,

One time a very funny thing happened. Baby

Alex was hungry. Aunt Jane asked, "Do you want to

First,

try feeding him." So we put Alex into his high chair.

Then ,and

We got out a jar of strained squash. I spooned some

into Alex's mouth. It came shooting right back out! It

my clothes. It was even in my hair.

got all over me. Alex made a funny face Aunt Jane

and I just laughed and laughed.

Checklist ✓
Revising

- Does your story suit your purpose and audience?

- Have you described your feelings clearly?

- Did you include enough details? Did you choose words carefully?

- Are the events in time order?

- Do the sentences flow easily when read aloud?

- Did you add a title?

PRACTICE AND APPLY
Revise Your Own Personal Narrative

1. Read your draft aloud to your partner. Listen to how it sounds.

2. Take notes on your partner's comments.

3. Use the notes from your peer conference to make your draft better.

4. Add a title.

21

Proofread/Edit

After you have revised your narrative, proofread it to find and correct any mistakes in mechanics, grammar and usage, and spelling.

STRATEGIES FOR PROOFREADING

- Reread your revised narrative, each time looking for a different type of mistake. **That way you will have a better chance of catching all mistakes.**

- Read for correct capitalization.

- Read for correct punctuation.

- Read aloud to check for sentence fragments.

- Check each word carefully to spot spelling mistakes.

TECHNOLOGY

Use the spell checker, but do not expect it to find every error. Read your draft carefully. Make sure that each word is the right word. For example, you may have typed "no" for "on" by mistake.

REVIEW THE RULES

GRAMMAR

- A sentence fragment is a group of words that does not express a complete thought. You can correct a sentence fragment by adding a subject or a predicate.

MECHANICS

- Every sentence begins with a capital letter.

- A statement ends with a period.

- A question ends with a question mark.

- A command ends with a period.

- An exclamation ends with an exclamation mark.

Go to pages 138–165 to review other rules.

Look at the proofreading corrections made on the draft below. What does the proofreading mark ⊙ mean? Why does the writer use that mark?

PREWRITE

DRAFT

REVISE

PROOFREAD

PUBLISH

PROOFREAD

My Aunt Jane

I love to visit   She
~~This is about~~ my Aunt Jane. ⋀Keeps me busy all

the time. We have a lot of fun together, even when
                    Best of all,
I make mistakes. ⋀She lets me try new things. She

~~even taught me how to swim.~~
When I visited Aunt Jane last summer,
    ~~One time~~ a very funny thing happened. Baby

Alex was hungry. Aunt Jane asked, "Do you want to
            ⌗First,
try feeding him?" So we put Alex into his high chair.
Then
We got out a jar of strained squash⋀ I spooned some
                                     and
into Alex's mouth. It came shooting right back out! It
        my clothes. It was even in my hair.
got all over me. Alex made a funny face⊙ Aunt Jane

and I just laughed and laughed.

Checklist ✓
Proofreading

- Did you spell all words correctly?

- Did you begin and end every sentence correctly?

- Is every sentence a complete thought?

- Did you indent the paragraphs?

PROOFREADING MARKS

⌗ new paragraph

⋀ add

ℭ take out

≡ Make a capital letter.

/ Make a small letter.

ⓈⓅ Check the spelling.

⊙ Add a period.

PRACTICE AND APPLY

Proofread Your Own Personal Narrative

1. Correct spelling mistakes.

2. Include end punctuation for each sentence.

3. Correct sentence fragments.

4. Indent paragraphs.

23

Writing PROCESS

Publish

Review your personal narrative one more time before you publish. Use this checklist.

✔ Self-Check Personal Narrative

❑ **Who was my audience? Did I write in a way that will interest and entertain them?**

❑ **What was my purpose? Did I share how I felt about my experience?**

❑ **Did I begin and end my story in an interesting way?**

❑ **Did I use time-order words to tell the order in which things happened?**

❑ **Did I write complete sentences? Do they fit together well?**

❑ **Did I proofread carefully and correct all mistakes?**

The writer used the checklist to review his narrative. Read "My Aunt Jane" and discuss it with your classmates. Was the piece ready to publish? Why or why not?

My Aunt Jane
by Timmy Chen

I love to visit my Aunt Jane. She keeps me busy all the time. We have a lot of fun together, even when I make mistakes. Best of all, she lets me try new things.

When I visited Aunt Jane last summer, a very funny thing happened. Baby Alex was hungry. Aunt Jane asked, "Do you want to try feeding him?"

First, we put Alex into his high chair. Then we got out a jar of strained squash, and I spooned some into Alex's mouth. It came shooting right back out! It got all over my clothes. It was even in my hair. Alex made a funny face. Aunt Jane and I just laughed and laughed.

PRACTICE AND APPLY

Publish Your Own Personal Narrative

1. Check your revised draft one more time.
2. Make a neat final copy.
3. Add a cover and some drawings or photos.

TIP!

TECHNOLOGY

Learn how to change the font in your word processing program. For your final copy, choose a font that is easy to read.

Personal Narrative

Score	Description
4 Excellent	■ tells about a personal experience and includes thoughts and feelings ■ includes a strong beginning and end ■ conveys a strong personal message ■ uses a variety of words in a natural way ■ uses a variety of sentences that flow ■ is free or almost free of errors
3 Good	■ tells about a personal experience and includes some thoughts and feelings ■ presents details in the correct order ■ makes an effort to share a message ■ uses appropriate words ■ uses a variety of complete sentences ■ has minor errors that do not confuse the reader
2 Fair	■ tells about a personal experience but loses focus ■ includes events told out of order ■ shows little personal involvement ■ does not use descriptive words or uses words poorly ■ uses only simple sentences ■ makes frequent errors that confuse the reader
1 Unsatisfactory	■ does not share a personal experience ■ tells events out of order and is confusing ■ does not express feelings or connect with readers ■ uses words not related to the purpose ■ uses run-on sentences and sentence fragments ■ makes serious and repeated errors

Go to www.macmillanmh.com for a 6-Point Student Writing Rubric.

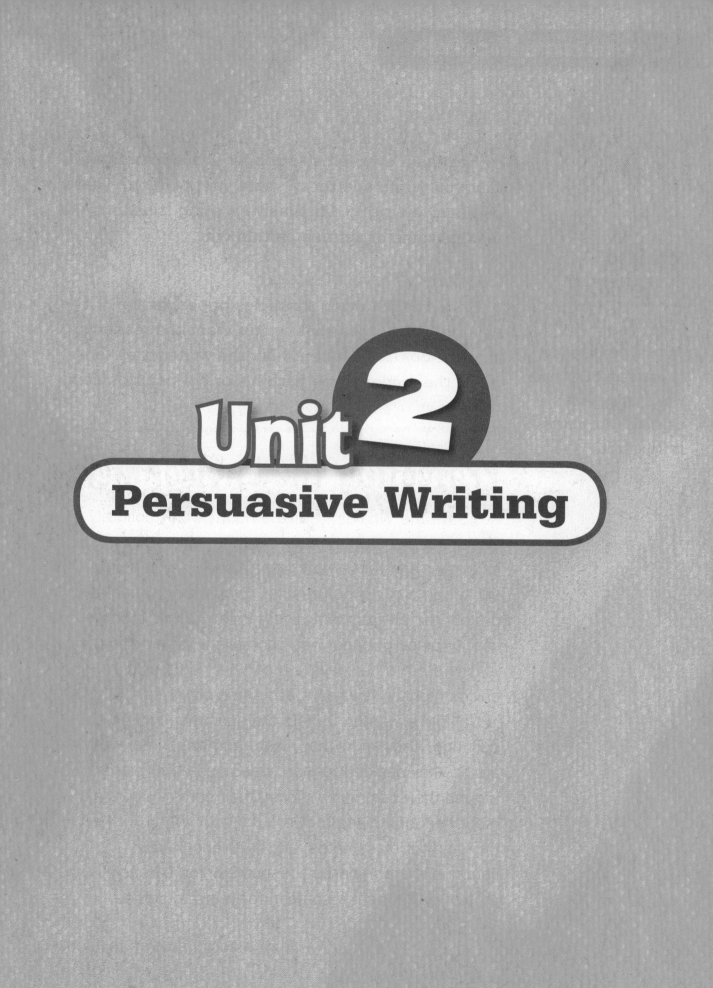

Unit 2

Persuasive Writing

Persuasive Writing

Have you ever felt so strongly about something that you wrote a letter to share your opinion? That's persuasive writing. Persuasive writing tries to make readers think or act in a certain way.

Learning from Writers

Read the following examples of persuasive writing. What does each writer want the reader to think or do? Think about how the writer tries to make the reader agree with his or her point of view.

THINK AND WRITE

Purpose
Why do people write to persuade? Explain why sharing your opinions with others is important.

Protecting the Environment

"Save the Whales." "Give a hoot...Don't pollute!" Protecting the environment and its resources is important and takes work. Just putting a bumper sticker on a car is not enough. Every day you can help protect the environment. Every time you use a bottle, can, or piece of paper, you can save it for recycling.

There are other ways you can help protect the environment. A few years ago some eight-year-old girls in California wanted to help their community fight air pollution. They knew that plants and trees improve the air. So they decided to plant trees and other plants around their community. Today their community is a more beautiful place to live.

You, your classmates, and everyone in your community are important resources. You can help protect our natural resources for years to come.

— from a social studies textbook

501 Paloma Road

San Diego, California 92129

September 4, 20_ _

Dear Mr. Scully,

I think Leo should win the award for the best pet-care report. He presented a wonderful report that made sense. The report explained what to do and why it was important. Leo even brought in his pet turtle Charlie to show us what he meant. Please give the award to Leo. Thank you.

Sincerely,

Amber Hawk

PRACTICE AND APPLY

Thinking Like a Reader

1. What does the writer of "Protecting the Environment" want readers to do?

2. Why does Amber believe that Leo should win the award?

Thinking Like a Writer

3. How are the writer's feelings stated in "Protecting the Environment"?

4. Why does Amber use facts to support her opinion?

5. **Reading Across Texts** Compare the two examples. How are they alike and how are they different in the way they try to persuade their readers?

Features of Persuasive Writing

DEFINITIONS AND FEATURES

Persuasive writing tries to make people think or act a certain way. Good persuasive writing:

▶ Clearly **states an opinion** about the topic.

▶ Supports the main idea with **convincing reasons and facts**.

▶ Organizes reasons in an **order that makes sense**.

▶ Uses **opinion words**.

▶ States an Opinion

Reread "Protecting the Environment" on page 28. How does the writer feel about the environment? What opinion does the writer have?

> Protecting the environment and its resources is important and takes work.

The word *important* tells you that the writer feels strongly about protecting the environment. The writer's opinion is stated clearly.

▶ Convincing Reasons and Facts

Convincing reasons and facts help persuade the reader. How does this suggestion persuade you that you can help protect the environment?

> Every time you use a bottle, can, or piece of paper, you can save it for recycling.

The suggestion shows how everyone can do simple things every day to help the environment.

▶ Order That Makes Sense

To help readers understand your ideas, put your supporting facts and reasons in an order that makes sense. After suggesting everyday things we can do, this writer introduced other ideas.

> There are other ways you can help protect the environment. A few years ago some eight-year-old girls in California wanted to help their community fight air pollution.

The writer gave readers everyday ideas before telling about a bigger project—planting trees and plants. Why did it make sense to "start small"?

▶ Opinion Words

Words such as *I think* and *I believe* signal the writer's opinion. *You can, must, need,* and *should* are opinion words writers use to persuade people to act.

> Every day you can help protect the environment.

What opinion words did the writer use?

PRACTICE AND APPLY

Create a Features Chart

1. List the features of persuasive writing.

2. Reread Amber Hawk's letter to Mr. Scully on page 29.

3. Write one example of each feature in Amber's writing.

4. Does Amber convince you? Explain why or why not.

Features	Examples

Prewrite

Writing PROCESS

Persuasive writing presents your opinion about something. Writing a persuasive letter gives you a chance to share your opinion with someone else.

Purpose and Audience

The purpose of persuasive writing is to explain what you think in a way that will persuade your reader to think or act in a certain way.

As you plan your persuasive letter, think about the reader. Whom are you trying to persuade? You need strong facts and reasons to get people to act.

Choose a Topic

Start by **brainstorming** a list of possible topics. Think of topics you have strong opinions about. From your list, choose a topic that you really believe in.

Once you choose a topic, **explore ideas** about it by listing reasons that support your opinions.

THINK **AND WRITE**

Audience
How will you persuade the reader to believe your idea is a good one? Write your answer.

These are good reasons to have a school newspaper.

School Newspaper
School doesn't have one.
Kids can write it.
We can share the work.
Families, friends, and neighbors
can read it.
I wonder what other
classes are doing.

Organize • Facts and Opinions

Opinions in a persuasive letter should be supported by facts and reasons. These ideas must be presented in an order that makes sense. A fact-and-opinion chart can help you organize your ideas. Look at how this writer organized her ideas as opinions and supporting reasons.

FACT-AND-OPINION CHART

Opinion Our school should have a newspaper.

Reason 1. We don't have one.

Reason 2. I wonder what other classes are doing.

Reason 3. Tell our families and town about our school.

Reason

Opinion Kids can write it.

Reason 1. Share the work.

Reason

Reason

Checklist ✓
Prewriting

- Did you list subjects you feel strongly about?

- Did you think about your purpose and the reader?

- Did you choose a topic?

- Did you use facts and reasons to support your opinions?

- Do you need to do any research?

PRACTICE AND APPLY

Plan Your Own Persuasive Letter

1. Think about your purpose and audience.

2. Brainstorm a list of topics.

3. Choose a topic and explore ideas about it.

4. Organize the facts and opinions.

Writing PROCESS

Prewrite • Research and Inquiry

▶ Writer's Resources

You may need to do research to get facts or ideas for your persuasive letter. First, make a list of questions. Then decide where you might find the answers.

What Else Do I Need to Know?	Where Can I Find the Information?
Who should write a school newspaper?	Library
What topics can students write about?	Periodicals

▶ Read Periodicals

Magazines and newspapers are called periodicals. They are good sources for up-to-date information. Your library may have a guide to periodicals that will lead you to newspaper or magazine articles on your subject.

STRATEGIES FOR USING PERIODICALS

- Prepare a list of possible topics or key words. You may need to search under more than one topic to find helpful articles.

- Ask the librarian to help you with your search.

- Take notes or make photocopies of pages with important information.

▶ Use Other Library Resources

Library resources can include books, magazines, CD-ROMs, videotapes, and other media. The reference librarian can show you how to find information on your topic in the card or computer catalog.

▶ Use Your Research

Information you find in your research can go in your chart. From her research, this writer learned that students can run a school newspaper. What other ideas did she discover?

Reason	1. We don't have one.
Reason	2. I wonder what other classes are doing.
Reason	3. Tell our families and town about our school.
Reason	4. A newspaper is the best way to let other people know what's going on.

Opinion	Kids can write it.
Reason	1. Share the work.
Reason	2. Classes can take turns being in charge.
Reason	3. Students can learn things from working on a newspaper.

Checklist ✔

Research and Inquiry

- Did you list your questions?

- Did you identify possible resources?

- Did you make notes?

PRACTICE AND APPLY

Review Your Plan

1. Look back at your prewriting chart.

2. List your questions.

3. Find out where you could look for answers.

4. Add new information you find to your chart.

Draft

Look at your chart before you begin to write your persuasive letter. Think about writing a paragraph for each opinion. Use your listed facts and reasons to support the opinion. Present your ideas in an order that makes sense.

This main idea is a good lead for the first paragraph.

FACT-AND-OPINION CHART

Opinion	Our school should have a newspaper.
Reason	1. We don't have one.
Reason	2. I wonder what other classes are doing.
Reason	3. Tell our families and town about our school.
Reason	4. A newspaper is the best way to let other people know what's going on.

Opinion	Kids can write it.
Reason	1. Share the work.
Reason	2. Classes can take turns being in charge.
Reason	3. Students can learn things from working on a newspaper.

Main idea for the second paragraph: Students can create the paper.

✓ Checklist

Drafting

- Does your letter fit your purpose and audience?

- Did you clearly state your opinions?

- Did you support your opinions with convincing reasons and facts?

- Are your opinions presented in an order that makes sense?

Look at how this writer turned ideas from the chart into paragraphs. First, she stated her idea for a school newspaper. Then she added supporting reasons.

DRAFT

September 14 20__

Dear Principal lin

The Brooksville School need a school newspaper
We don't have one. a newspaper will help us learn
about each other. I wonder what other classes are
doing. I want to read about everything. To tell our
families and Town.

A school newspaper can help students. They
can do things together. Students can write. They
can publish the newspaper Clases can take turns
being in charge. A newspaper is important.

Sincerely,

Alisha Beal

Main idea: The school needs a school newspaper.

These reasons explain why the writer thinks the school should have a newspaper.

These details tell how students can create the newspaper.

TECHNOLOGY

Find out how to change the space between lines on the computer. If you use double space for your draft, you'll have room to make changes.

PRACTICE AND APPLY

Draft Your Own Persuasive Letter

1. Look again at your prewriting chart.

2. Clearly state your opinions.

3. Support your opinions with facts and reasons.

Revise

Elaborate

You can improve your writing by elaborating. When you elaborate, you add important details. As you revise your persuasive letter, you may need to add facts or reasons to support your opinions.

This writer added details to make her reasons for wanting a newspaper clearer.

> I wonder what other classes are doing.
>
> their projects and trips.
> I want to read about ~~everything.~~

Here the writer explained how working on a newspaper could help students.

> will teach us how to work
> A school newspaper ~~can help students. They~~
>
> ~~can do things~~ together.

Word Choice

When you write, choose words that will help make your opinion clear.

In a persuasive letter, opinion words attract the reader's attention. They help focus the reader on your ideas and show the reader that you believe in your ideas.

> We ought to know
> ~~I wonder~~ what other classes are doing.

OPINION WORDS

I believe
I think
would be better
should
know
must
need
ought
require
want
agree

Better Sentences

When you revise, look at your sentences. Listen to them as you read your letter aloud. Do your sentences fit together? Have you included different kinds of sentences?

Sometimes you can combine two sentences with the same subject by joining the two predicates.

Students can write. ~~They can~~ *the articles and* publish the newspaper.

PRACTICE AND APPLY

Revise Your Own Persuasive Letter

1. Add details or reasons to support your opinions.

2. Listen to your opening statement. Does it clearly state your opinion?

3. Add opinion words to persuade your readers.

4. **Grammar** Are there some sentences that you should combine?

TECHNOLOGY

Use the header feature to put your name, class, and date at the top of every page.

Revise • Peer Conferencing

Trade your first draft with a partner. Read each other's writing. Then ask each other for ideas.

Writing PROCESS

September 14 20__

Dear Principal lin

[The Brooksville School need a school newspaper We don't have one. a newspaper will help us learn about each other. I wonder what other classes are doing. I want to read about everything. To tell our families and Town.

A school newspaper can help students. They can do things together. Students can write. They can publish the newspaper Clases can take turns being in charge. A newspaper is important.

Sincerely,

Alisha Beal

A school newspaper is a great idea!

You don't need this sentence.

What do you want Mr. Lin to do?

TiP!

Conferencing for the Reader

- Did your partner include these features of a persuasive letter?
  - clear statement of opinion
  - supporting reasons and facts given in an order that makes sense
  - opinion words
- Make suggestions. Also tell your partner what you like about the letter.

Revise your letter using your partner's comments and suggestions. How did this writer do it?

REVISE

September 14 20___

Dear Principal lin

The Brooksville School need a school newspaper

~~We don't have one.~~ a newspaper will help us learn
We ought to know
about each other. ~~I wonder~~ what other classes are
, such as their projects and trips. We need
doing. ~~I want to read about everything.~~ To tell our
about our school
families and Town.

will teach us how to work
A school newspaper ~~can help students.~~ They
We ^ *the articles and*
~~can do things~~ together. ~~Students~~ can write. They
ourselves.
~~can~~ publish the newspaper. Clases can take turns
Please let us start our school newspaper.
being in charge. ~~A newspaper is important.~~

Sincerely,

Alisha Beal

Checklist ✓
Revising

- Does your letter fit your purpose and audience?

- Do your sentences fit together well?

- Are your opinions supported by facts?

- Have you used opinion words to help persuade your audience?

- Is your opening statement strong?

PRACTICE AND APPLY
Revise Your Own Persuasive Letter

1. Read your letter aloud to your partner.

2. Use your notes from the peer conference to make your draft better.

3. Make your opening statement strong.

Proofread/Edit

Writing PROCESS

You need to proofread your revised letter. Correct mistakes in mechanics, grammar and usage, and spelling.

STRATEGIES FOR PROOFREADING

- Reread your letter several times. **Look for a different kind of error each time.**

- Look for errors in capitalization and punctuation.

- Make sure singular and plural nouns are spelled correctly.

- Use a dictionary or computer spell checker for spelling mistakes.

TiP!

TECHNOLOGY

Print a copy of your letter. It's easier to check mistakes on paper than on the computer screen.

REVIEW THE RULES

GRAMMAR

- A singular noun names one person, place, or thing. A plural noun names more than one.

- Add -s to form the plural of most nouns.

- Add -es to form the plural of nouns that end in s, sh, ch, or x.

MECHANICS

- Use a comma between the name of a city or town and the state.

- Use a comma between the day and the year in a date.

- Capitalize the first word of the greeting and the closing in a letter.

- Use a comma after the greeting and the closing in a letter.

Go to pages 138–165 to review other rules.

Look at the proofreading corrections made on the draft. What does the proofreading mark / mean?

PROOFREAD

September 14, 20__

Dear Principal lin,

The Brooksville School need a school newspaper.
                                    s

We don't have one. a newspaper will help us learn
We ought to know
about each other. I wonder what other classes are
         , such as their projects and trips. We need
doing. I want to read about everything. To tell our
              about our school
families and Town.
                              will teach us how to work
      A school newspaper can help students. They
                         We
can do things together. Students can write. They
                       , the articles and
                  ourselves. Classes
can publish the newspaper. Clases can take turns
Please let us start our school newspaper.
being in charge. A newspaper is important.

                              Sincerely,

                              Alisha Beal

Checklist ✓
Proofreading

- Did you use commas correctly?

- Did you indent each paragraph?

- Did you capitalize all proper nouns?

- Did you spell all words correctly?

PROOFREADING MARKS

⌗	new paragraph
∧	add
℘	take out
=	Make a capital letter.
/	Make a small letter.
SP	Check spelling.
⊙	Add a period.

PRACTICE AND APPLY

Proofread Your Own Persuasive Letter

1. Check for proper use of singular and plural nouns.

2. Use commas in the greeting, closing, and date.

3. Correct spelling mistakes.

43

Publish

Look at your persuasive letter one more time before you publish it. A list like the one below can help you check your writing.

✓ **Self-Check**   Persuasive Letter

❑ **What is my purpose? Will the reader understand my ideas?**

❑ **Did I explain my ideas so that the reader will agree with them?**

❑ **Did I use opinion words to make my position clear?**

❑ **Did I support my opinions with reasons and facts?**

❑ **Do my sentences fit together well?**

❑ **Are my ideas presented in an order that makes sense?**

❑ **Did I proofread and correct all mistakes?**

This writer used the checklist to look over her writing. Think about her ideas as you read the letter. Do you think the letter is ready to be published? Why or why not?

September 14, 20_ _

Dear Principal Lin,

The Brooksville School needs a school newspaper. A newspaper will help us learn about each other. We ought to know what other classes are doing, such as their projects and trips. We need to tell our families and town about our school.

A school newspaper will teach us how to work together. We can write the articles and publish the newspaper ourselves. Classes can take turns being in charge. Please let us start our school newspaper.

Sincerely,
Alisha Beal

PRACTICE AND APPLY

Publish Your Own Persuasive Writing

1. Check your revised draft one more time.

2. Make a neat final copy.

3. Add drawings or photographs.

TIP!

TECHNOLOGY

Does your school have a web site? You might want to publish your letter at the web site for other classes to read.

Persuasive Writing

Score	Description
4 Excellent	■ presents a clear opinion with supporting details ■ presents reasons in a logical order ■ shows strong interest in the issue and connects to readers ■ uses opinion words and new vocabulary ■ uses a variety of sentences that flow ■ is free or almost free of errors
3 Good	■ presents a clear opinion with supporting details ■ presents reasons for an opinion in a logical order ■ shows interest in the issue and connects to readers ■ uses opinion words ■ uses a variety of complete sentences ■ has minor errors that do not confuse the reader
2 Fair	■ attempts to present an opinion, but supporting details are weak ■ presents reasons for the opinion, but not in a logical order ■ shows little connection with readers ■ uses only one or two opinion words ■ is choppy and awkward ■ makes frequent errors that confuse the reader
1 Unsatisfactory	■ does not present an opinion ■ is poorly organized with disconnected ideas ■ is dull and unconvincing ■ uses words not connected to the purpose ■ uses run-on sentences and sentence fragments ■ makes serious and repeated errors

Go to www.macmillanmh.com for a 6-Point Student Writing Rubric.

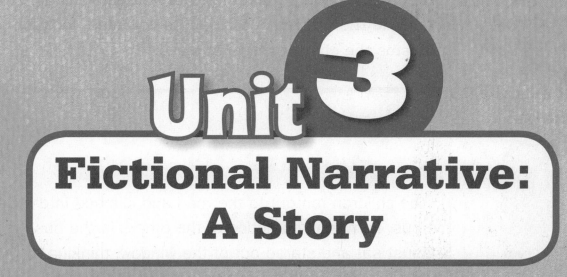

Unit 3

Fictional Narrative: A Story

A Story

A story can be about anyone and anything. When you write a story, you can use your imagination to create interesting, entertaining characters and events. Your story can tell how the characters solve their problems.

Learning from Writers

Read the following examples of stories. What events do the writers describe? As you read, look for problems the characters must solve.

THINK AND WRITE

Purpose

Why do you think people write stories? Why do you think other people like to read them? Write a brief explanation.

A Name for a Pig

The children ran out to the road and climbed into the bus. Fern took no notice of the others in the bus. She just sat and stared out of the window, thinking what a blissful world it was and how lucky she was to have entire charge of a pig. By the time the bus reached school, Fern had named her pet, selecting the most beautiful name she could think of.

"Its name is Wilbur," she whispered to herself.

She was still thinking about the pig when the teacher said, "Fern, what is the capital of Pennsylvania?"

"Wilbur," replied Fern, dreamily. The pupils giggled. Fern blushed.

—E. B. White, from *Charlotte's Web*

The Thinking Cap

Max's big sister was so smart that she could do her homework just by looking at it. Max wasn't like that. He had to work and work.

"Put on your thinking cap," everyone told him.

"I wish I had a thinking cap," said Max sadly as he walked home from school.

Just then, Max saw a red hat on the path. He picked up the hat and put it on. "I have 500 meters left to go," he thought. How strange! He hardly knew what a meter was!

Max wore the hat home. His mother was cooking. "If you double that recipe, you'll need $3\frac{1}{2}$ cups of flour," said Max. His mother dropped her spoon.

Max wore the hat to school. In no time, his teacher saw that Max should graduate and go to college. At graduation, people wore black caps with tassels. Max wore his red hat.

— Robbie Clifford

PRACTICE AND APPLY

Thinking Like a Reader

1. Name an event from the beginning, middle, and end of E. B. White's story.

2. How was Max's problem solved in "The Thinking Cap"?

Thinking Like a Writer

3. How did E. B. White get you interested in reading his story from beginning to end?

4. How did the author of "The Thinking Cap" present the problem and solution?

5. **Reading Across Texts** How are the characters in the two stories alike and different?

Features of a Story

DEFINITIONS AND FEATURES

Stories can be make-believe or real. A good story:

▸ Has an interesting **beginning, middle, and end**.

▸ Has a **plot** with a problem that needs to be solved.

▸ Has **characters** who make things happen and a **setting** where the action takes place.

▸ Uses **describing words** to tell about the characters, setting, and events.

▸ Beginning, Middle, and End

The beginning of a story tells what the story will be about. The middle of the story tells what happens. The end of the story tells how everything turns out. Reread "A Name for a Pig" on page 48.

> The children ran out to the road and climbed into the bus. Fern took no notice of the others in the bus.

How does this beginning grab your attention?

▸ Plot

The events of the plot show the character's problem and how it is solved.

> By the time the bus reached school, Fern had named her pet, selecting the most beautiful name she could think of.

This solution may make you wonder what name Fern has chosen for her pet.

► Characters and Setting

The people in a story are called characters. The setting is where a story takes place. The sentence below introduces the main character of "A Name for a Pig" and shows how she is feeling.

> Fern took no notice of the others in the bus. She just sat and stared out of the window, thinking what a blissful world it was and how lucky she was to have entire charge of a pig.

Where is Fern? What is she feeling?

► Describing Words

To help readers form a clear picture in their minds of story characters, settings, and events, writers use describing words such as adjectives and adverbs.

> "Wilbur," replied Fern, dreamily.

What describing word did the author use to show how Fern replied?

PRACTICE AND APPLY

Create a Features Chart

1. List the features of a good story.

2. Reread "The Thinking Cap" by Robbie Clifford on page 49.

3. Write one example of each feature in Robbie's writing.

4. Write what you thought was the funniest part of Robbie's story.

Features	Examples

Prewrite

Writing PROCESS

A story can be make-believe or real. Writing a story lets you use your imagination and be creative.

Purpose and Audience

The purpose of writing a story is to express your ideas and entertain your audience.

Before writing, you need to think about your audience. Who will be reading your story? How will you present your ideas to your readers?

Choose a Topic

Begin by **brainstorming** a list of topics. Remember that there are many kinds of stories. From your list, choose a topic that would make an enjoyable story for your readers.

After you have chosen a topic, **explore ideas** about characters, a setting, a story problem, and events you might include in your story. This writer decided to write a tall tale about a character who is larger than life and can do amazing things.

THINK AND WRITE

Audience
How can you give your audience a clear picture of your characters? Write your ideas in your journal.

Here is how I explored my ideas.

My character is a giant woman.
She's very strong and powerful.
Too big for her home
Needs a bigger place to live
Lives in Texas
Can lasso things with her rope
Can walk across state in a
   few minutes
Changes size of the state

Organize • Beginning, Middle, and End

A good story has a beginning, middle, and end. The writer introduces the main character and a problem in the beginning. In the middle, the writer shows how the character tries to solve the problem. Then the writer tells what happens at the end. To plan your story, you can use a story map.

PREWRITE

DRAFT

REVISE

PROOFREAD

PUBLISH

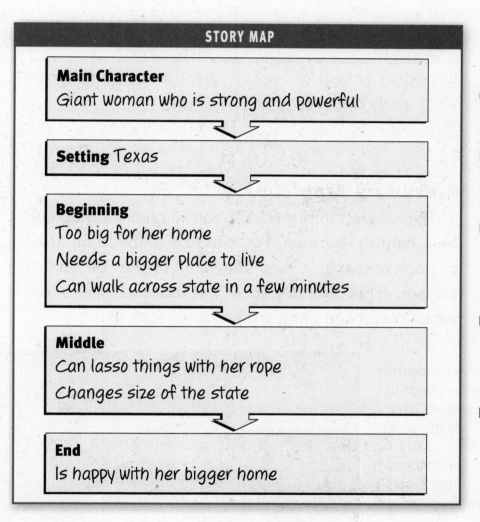

STORY MAP

Main Character
Giant woman who is strong and powerful

Setting Texas

Beginning
Too big for her home
Needs a bigger place to live
Can walk across state in a few minutes

Middle
Can lasso things with her rope
Changes size of the state

End
Is happy with her bigger home

Checklist ✓
Prewriting

■ Have you thought about your purpose and audience?

■ Have you decided what type of story to write and chosen a topic?

■ Have you thought about characters, setting, and a story problem?

■ Are your ideas organized in a chart that tells the beginning, middle, and end of your story?

■ Do you need to do any research?

PRACTICE AND APPLY

Plan Your Own Personal Narrative

1. Decide on a type of story.

2. Brainstorm and explore story ideas.

3. Organize your ideas.

Prewrite • Research and Inquiry

▶ Writer's Resources

You may have to do research to get more information for your story. First, make a list of questions you have. Next, decide what resources you can use to find the answers.

What Else Do I Need to Know?	Where Can I Find the Information?
What does Texas look like?	Check a map of the United States.
What words can I use to describe my character?	Look in a thesaurus.

▶ Study a Map

If you need information about a place, a map can be a helpful resource. You can find maps in an *atlas*, or book of maps. A map shows all or part of Earth's surface. This map of part of the United States shows what Texas and some other states look like.

The key explains the meanings of symbols used on the map.

The compass rose shows where north is.

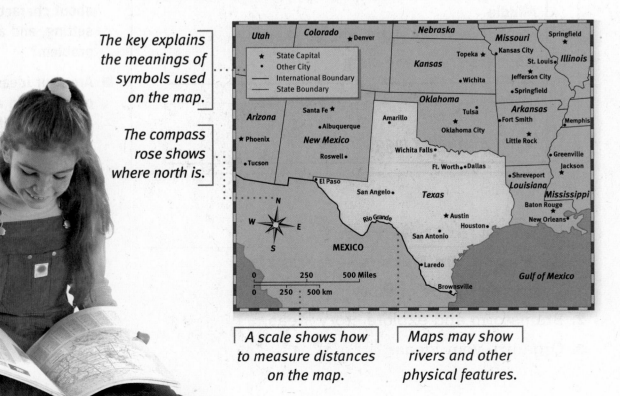

A scale shows how to measure distances on the map.

Maps may show rivers and other physical features.

▶ Use a Thesaurus

A thesaurus is a special kind of dictionary that lists synonyms, or words that have almost the same meaning. It also lists antonyms, which are words with opposite meanings. You can use a thesaurus when you don't want to use the same word over and over.

Use Your Research

You can include in your story map new information gathered from your research. This writer learned important information from studying a map and using a thesaurus. How did she change her story map?

Beginning
Too big for her home < large, huge, enormous, gigantic
Needs a bigger place to live
Can walk across state in a few minutes

Middle
Can lasso things with her rope
Changes size of the state – and shape

End —Texas is quite wide in the middle.
Is happy with her bigger home

Checklist ✓

Research and Inquiry

- Did you list questions about your topic?

- Did you identify resources to use?

- Did you take notes?

PRACTICE and APPLY

Review Your Plan

1. Look at your prewriting chart.

2. List questions you have about your topic.

3. Identify the resources you will need to use.

4. Add new information you gather to your chart.

Draft

Before you begin writing your story, review the story map you made. Think about making a paragraph for each part of the story.

STORY MAP

Main Character
Giant woman who is strong and powerful

Setting Texas

Beginning
Too big for her home < large, huge, enormous, gigantic
Needs a bigger place to live
Can walk across state in a few minutes

Middle
Can lasso things with her rope
Changes size of the state — and shape

End —— Texas is quite wide in the middle.
Is happy with her bigger home

First paragraph: Introduces the character and her problem

Second paragraph: How the character solves the problem

Third paragraph: What happens at the end

✓ Checklist

Drafting

- Does your story fit your purpose and audience?

- Did you introduce the characters at the beginning?

- Does your story have a plot with a problem that needs to be solved?

- Have you written an interesting beginning, middle, and end?

- Did you include details that will help readers picture what is happening?

Look at how this writer used the ideas in her story map to write a draft.

PREWRITE

DRAFT

REVISE

PROOFREAD

PUBLISH

DRAFT

Too-Tall Tilly lived in Texas. Too-Tall Tilly was almost as big as Texas. She had a big horse, too. She was so large that she could walk across the whole state in a few giant steps.

This state is too small for me, Too-Tall Tilly said. So she tied a rope around one side of the state. She yanked and pulled. That side of the state stretched and stretched. Then Too-Tall Tilly leaped to the other side of the state. She tied the rope to it and yanked and pulled. that side of the state stretched out, too. Too-Tall Tilly kept stretching the state. It's big enough for me now, she shouted. And that is why Texas is so wide in the middle.

The main character is introduced and described at the beginning.

The problem that needs to be solved is stated.

Plot events in the middle tell how the character solves her problem.

The story ends in an interesting way.

TECHNOLOGY

When you write on the computer, remember to save your work often. Give your document a name that will help you remember what it is about and when it was written.

PRACTICE AND APPLY

Draft Your Own Story

1. Review your prewriting chart.

2. Write about a problem that needs to be solved.

3. Give your story a beginning, middle, and end.

Revise

Elaborate

You can improve your writing by elaborating. When you elaborate, you add important ideas and details that may be missing from your writing. When you revise your story, you may need to add more details to create a picture for the reader.

The writer added a detail that explains why Texas is important to her tall tale.

Too-Tall Tilly lived in Texas. , which is a big state

The next detail the writer added helps the reader understand what happened to the state.

Soon Texas was the size it is today.

Too-Tall Tilly kept stretching the state.

Word Choice

When you write, it is important to choose just the right words for your topic and audience.

In a story, you need to use colorful, interesting words to describe settings, characters, and actions.

This state is too small for me, Too-Tall Tilly grumbled glumly said.

DESCRIBING WORDS

huge
floppy
swift
funny
delicious
cheerful
loudly
eagerly
slowly
carefully
brightly
rapidly

Better Paragraphs

As you revise your draft, check your paragraphs to make sure each paragraph contains just one main idea. Details in the paragraph should support that main idea.

Sometimes you may need to move sentences from one paragraph to another.

She was so large that she could walk across the whole state in a few giant steps. ∧

This state is too small for me, Too-Tall Tilly ~~grumbled glumly~~
~~said.~~
∧

TECHNOLOGY

Use the FIND AND REPLACE feature when you want to replace a word that you have used several times in your draft.

PRACTICE AND APPLY

Revise Your Own Story

1. Add details or information that will make your writing clearer or more interesting.

2. Use colorful and exact words that will create a clear picture for the reader.

3. Take out information that is not necessary.

4. **Grammar** Can you combine two sentences that tell about the same person, place, or thing?

Revise • Peer Conferencing

Give a copy of your first draft to a partner to read. Read your partner's draft. You may be able to offer each other some fresh ideas.

Writing PROCESS

Too-Tall Tilly lived in Texas. Too-Tall Tilly was almost as big as Texas. She had a big horse, too. She was so large that she could walk across the whole state in a few giant steps.

This state is too small for me, Too-Tall Tilly said. So she tied a rope around one side of the state. She yanked and pulled. That side of the state stretched and stretched. Then Too-Tall Tilly leaped to the other side of the state. She tied the rope to it and yanked and pulled. that side of the state stretched out, too. Too-Tall Tilly kept stretching the state. It's big enough for me now, she shouted.

And that is why Texas is so wide in the middle.

What does Too-Tall Tilly look like?

This part about the horse isn't necessary.

Good ending for a tall tale!

TiP!

Conferencing for the Reader

- Are features of a story included in your partner's draft?
  - an interesting beginning, middle, and end
  - a plot with a problem
  - characters who make things happen
  - describing words
- Tell what you like about the draft.

When you revise your story, think about the suggestions your partner made. This writer made some changes based on her partner's ideas.

REVISE

Too-Tall Tilly
^

,which is a big state

Too-Tall Tilly lived in Texas. Too-Tall Tilly was
^
She had broad shoulders and strong arms. ?
almost as big as Texas. ~~She had a big horse, too.~~
^

She was so large that she could walk across the

whole state in a few giant steps.
^
grumbled glumly

This state is too small for me, Too-Tall Tilly ~~said~~.
^

So she tied a rope around one side of the state.

She yanked and pulled. That side of the state

stretched and stretched. Then Too-Tall Tilly leaped

to the other side of the state. She tied the rope

to it and yanked and pulled. that side of the state

stretched out, too. Too-Tall Tilly kept stretching the
Soon Texas was the size it is today.   happily
state. It's big enough for me now, she shouted.
^   ^

And that is why Texas is so wide in the middle.

Checklist ✔
Revising

- Does your story suit your purpose and audience?

- Do you need to elaborate on any part of your story?

- Does your story have a clear beginning, middle, and end?

- Did you use colorful words?

- Do the sentences flow smoothly when read aloud?

- Did you add a title?

PRACTICE AND APPLY
Revise Your Own Story

1. Take notes on your partner's comments.

2. Use your notes to improve your draft.

3. Add a title.

Proofread/Edit

After you have revised your story, you should proofread it. You need to correct any errors in mechanics, grammar and usage, and spelling.

STRATEGIES FOR PROOFREADING

- Reread your revised story, each time looking for a different type of mistake. You'll have a better chance of catching all the errors.

- Check each sentence for correct capitalization.

- Reread for correct end punctuation.

- Look for quotation marks at the beginning and end of a person's exact words.

- Check for spelling mistakes.

TiP!

TECHNOLOGY

Do you sometimes forget to indent paragraphs? Word processing programs usually let you set margins so that the first line of a paragraph indents automatically.

REVIEW THE RULES

GRAMMAR

- A verb must agree with the time of the action. A present-tense verb tells what is happening now. A past-tense verb tells about a past action. A future-tense verb tells about an action that is going to happen.

MECHANICS

- Use a comma after the name of a person being spoken to.

- Use a comma after words such as *yes* and *no* when they begin a sentence.

- Use quotation marks at the beginning and end of a person's exact words.

Go to pages 138–165 to review other rules.

Look at the proofreading corrections made on the draft below. What does the proofreading mark ¶ mean? Why does the writer use this mark?

PREWRITE

DRAFT

REVISE

PROOFREAD

PUBLISH

PROOFREAD

Too-Tall Tilly

,which is a big state

Too-Tall Tilly lived in Texas. Too-Tall Tilly was

She had broad shoulders and strong arms.

almost as big as Texas. She had a big horse, too.

She was so large that she could walk across the

whole state in a few giant steps.

grumbled glumly

"This state is too small for me," Too-Tall Tilly said.

So she tied a rope around one side of the state.

She yanked and pulled. That side of the state

stretched and stretched. Then Too-Tall Tilly leaped

to the other side of the state. She tied the rope to

it and yanked and pulled. that side of the state

stretched out, too. Too-Tall Tilly kept stretching the

Soon Texas was the size it is today.   happily

state. "It's big enough for me now," she shouted.

¶ And that is why Texas is so wide in the middle.

Checklist ✓
Proofreading

- **Did you spell all words correctly?**

- **Did you begin each sentence with a capital letter?**

- **Did you indent each paragraph?**

- **Did you use quotation marks correctly?**

PROOFREADING MARKS

¶	new paragraph
^	add
℘	take out
≡	Make a capital letter.
/	Make a small letter.
SP	Check spelling.
⊙	Add a period.

PRACTICE AND APPLY

Proofread Your Own Story

1. Correct spelling mistakes.

2. Use quotation marks where needed.

3. Indent paragraphs.

Writing PROCESS

Publish

Before you publish, review your story one more time. A checklist can help you.

✓ **Self-Check** Story

☐ **Who is my audience? Did I write about something that will interest them?**

☐ **What is my purpose? Will readers be entertained?**

☐ **Did I write an interesting beginning, middle, and end?**

☐ **Does my plot have a problem to be solved?**

☐ **Did I choose good describing words and details to tell about the characters, setting, and events?**

☐ **Do I like the sound of my story when I read it aloud? Do the sentences flow smoothly?**

☐ **Did I proofread and correct all mistakes?**

The writer used the checklist to review her story. Read "Too-Tall Tilly" and discuss the writer's published piece. Was it ready to be published? Discuss why or why not.

Too-Tall Tilly

by Debbie Griffin

Too-Tall Tilly lived in Texas, which is a big state. Too-Tall Tilly was almost as big as Texas. She had broad shoulders and strong arms. She was so large that she could walk across the whole state in a few giant steps. "This state is too small for me," Too-Tall Tilly grumbled glumly.

So she tied a rope around one side of the state. She yanked and pulled. That side of the state stretched and stretched. Then Too-Tall Tilly leaped to the other side of the state. She tied the rope to it and yanked and pulled. That side of the state stretched out, too. Too-Tall Tilly kept stretching the state. Soon Texas was the size it is today. "It's big enough for me now!" she shouted happily.

And that is why Texas is so wide in the middle.

PRACTICE AND APPLY

Publish Your Own Story

1. Check your revised draft one last time.

2. Make a neat copy of your draft.

3. Add a border, pictures, or a cover.

TiP!

Handwriting

When you make your final copy, leave some space between the title and the rest of the story. Remember to indent the first line of each paragraph.

	A Story
Score	**Description**
4 Excellent	▪ creates an entertaining, detailed story ▪ moves readers through an engaging beginning, middle, and end ▪ uses an original voice and well-crafted dialogue ▪ uses advanced vocabulary ▪ uses a variety of sentences that flow ▪ is free or almost free of errors
3 Good	▪ creates a solid, detailed story ▪ creates a clear beginning, middle, and end ▪ attempts to create a personal style ▪ uses both new and everyday words ▪ includes easy-to-follow sentences ▪ has minor errors that do not confuse the reader
2 Fair	▪ attempts to create a story with some details ▪ has an unclear beginning, middle, and end ▪ lacks involvement with readers ▪ uses words that are unclear ▪ includes sentences that are understandable but awkward ▪ makes frequent errors that confuse the reader
1 Unsatisfactory	▪ does not tell a story ▪ has no beginning, middle, or end ▪ shows no engagement with readers ▪ uses words not connected to the purpose ▪ uses run-on sentences and sentence fragments ▪ makes serious and repeated errors

Go to www.macmillanmh.com for a 6-Point Student Writing Rubric.

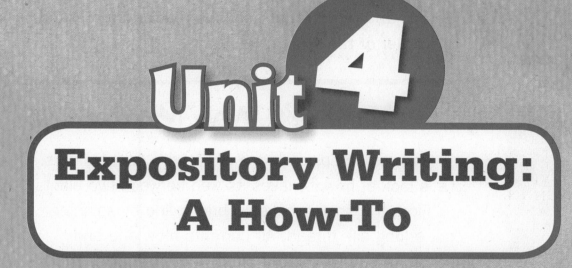

Unit 4
Expository Writing: A How-To

How-to Writing

Have you ever told someone how to do or make something? How-to writing explains how to do something step by step.

Learning from Writers

Read the following examples of explanatory writing. What do the writers explain? How did they organize their writing? As you read, look for exact details and words that help the reader understand the order of the steps.

THINK AND WRITE

Purpose

Why do you think people write and read instructions? Write your answer in your journal.

Nature's Web Maker

The garden spider is one of nature's best builders. Let's look at how it makes its web between two plants.

First, the spider makes a bridge line by spinning out a long silk thread. Air currents blow one end of this thread to another plant where it sticks. The spider travels along the bridge line it has made. It drops another line down to a plant below and travels down it. Then it comes back up with another silk thread to make a triangle. The spider keeps spinning. Back and forth, up and down, the spider goes. The web now looks something like the spokes of a wheel. Then the spider lays the trap—a long thread of sticky silk that spirals around the spokes until it reaches the center of the wheel. When the spider gets a victim, it can race down the spokes because they are dry, not sticky, and capture its prey.

—Diane Hoyt-Goldsmith, from *Spiders at Work*

How to Plan a Family Picnic

You can have a good family picnic if you follow some simple steps. First, pick the perfect spot. This might be a park or a lake. Second, make sure that everyone will like the food on the menu. It would be awful to spend all that time cooking and find out that your cousins hate chicken! Third, give everyone a little job to do. If Uncle Harry is minding the little kids, they won't stick their fingers in the pies. Fourth, serve the food before everyone gets too hungry. Finally, make sure everyone at the picnic helps clean up. Follow these rules, and your family will have a lot of fun.

— Miguel Santos

PRACTICE AND APPLY

Thinking Like a Reader

1. In "Nature's Web Maker," how does the spider begin its web?

2. How many steps are explained in "How to Plan a Family Picnic"? Name them.

Thinking Like a Writer

3. In "Nature's Web Maker," what details are used to make the first step clear?

4. How did the author of "How to Plan a Family Picnic" make the order of the steps clear?

5. **Reading Across Texts** Compare how the instructions in the two samples are organized. Tell what is the same and what is different.

Features of How-to Writing

DEFINITIONS AND FEATURES

A How-to gives directions or explains how to do something. Good explanatory writing:

► Tells **how to** complete a specific task.

► Presents **step-by-step instructions**.

► Gives **clear details** that are easy to follow.

► Uses **time-order** or **space-order words** to make instructions clear.

► How To

Reread "Nature's Web Maker" by Diane Hoyt-Goldsmith on page 68. What specific task does the author explain?

> The garden spider is one of nature's best builders. Let's look at how it makes its web between two plants.

The first two sentences tell what the writing will explain.

► Step-by-Step Instructions

When you write instructions, the steps need to be in the order they are carried out.

> First, the spider makes a bridge line by spinning out a long silk thread. Air currents blow one end of this thread to another plant where it sticks.

What time-order word helps make the steps easier to follow?

▶ Clear Details

Exact details help your readers understand each step. The sentence below describes how the web looks.

> The web now looks something like the spokes of a wheel.

Can you picture in your mind exactly how the web looks?

▶ Space-Order Words

Sometimes it is just as important to show *where* something takes place as *when* it takes place. To help your readers clearly understand directions, use space-order words, such as *up*, *across*, *between*, *in front of*, and *under*.

> The spider travels along the bridge line it has made. It drops another line down to a plant below and travels down it.

What space-order words did the author use?

PRACTICE AND APPLY

Create a Features Chart

1. List the features of good how-to writing.

2. Reread "How to Plan a Family Picnic" by Miguel Santos on page 69.

3. Write one example of each feature in Miguel's writing.

4. Write the feature of Miguel's writing that was most helpful to you in following the instructions.

Features	Examples

Prewrite

How-to writing gives directions or explains how to do or make something. Writing how-to instructions gives you a chance to share what you know how to do.

Purpose and Audience

The purpose of writing instructions is to explain how to complete a task step by step.

Think about your audience before you begin to write. Who will be following your directions? How can you make them easy to understand?

Choose a Topic

Begin by **brainstorming** a list of things you know how to do well. Choose a topic your readers might be interested in.

After choosing your topic, **explore ideas** by listing the steps to follow. Think about the order of each step.

THINK AND WRITE

Audience
How can you help your readers follow the directions? Write your answer.

I explored my ideas by listing the steps.

A Cake for Birds

Get foods birds like.

Mix them together.

Press them into a cake.

Chill the cake.

Put it outside.

Organize • Sequence

When you explain how to do something, you write the steps in a certain order, or sequence. To plan your instructions, you can use a sequence chart. Start with a sentence that helps your audience understand your purpose. List in order the steps you need to follow. What idea has this writer added to his chart?

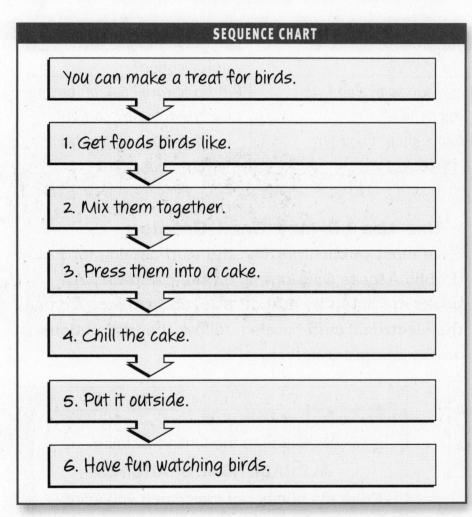

SEQUENCE CHART

You can make a treat for birds.

1. Get foods birds like.

2. Mix them together.

3. Press them into a cake.

4. Chill the cake.

5. Put it outside.

6. Have fun watching birds.

PRACTICE AND APPLY

Plan Your Own Instructions

1. Brainstorm ideas for a topic.

2. Think about your purpose and audience.

3. Choose a topic.

4. Organize the details in step-by-step order.

Checklist ✔
Prewriting

- Have you thought about your purpose and audience?

- Have you chosen a topic and explored ideas about it?

- Are your ideas organized in a chart?

- Did you begin by stating your purpose?

- Have you checked the order of the steps?

- Do you need to do any research?

Prewrite • Research and Inquiry

▶ Writer's Resources

You may need to do some research to get more information for your instructions. First, make a list of your questions. Then decide what resources you need in order to answer your questions.

What Else Do I Need to Know?	Where Can I Find the Information?
What kinds of food do birds like?	Find a library book on birds. Use the table of contents
Where should you put the cake?	or the index to locate information.

▶ Use the Library Card Catalog

In most public libraries, the card catalog, or PAC (Public Access Catalog), is on the computer. All books are listed by author, title, and subject. To use the electronic card catalog, follow the instructions on the computer screen.

If you want to find books about one subject, such as birds, use this search.

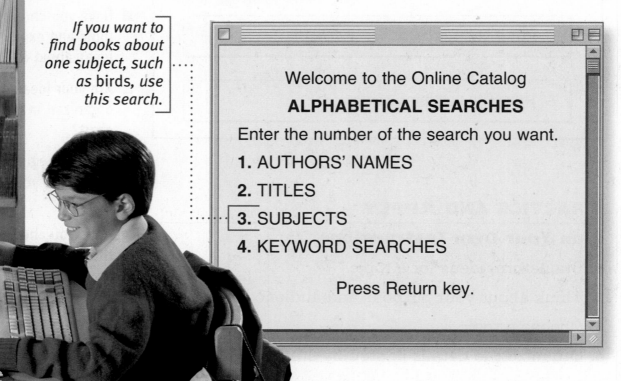

Welcome to the Online Catalog

ALPHABETICAL SEARCHES

Enter the number of the search you want.

1. AUTHORS' NAMES

2. TITLES

3. SUBJECTS

4. KEYWORD SEARCHES

Press Return key.

► Use Parts of a Book

The table of contents appears at the front of a book. It lists the titles and beginning page numbers of all the sections of the book. An index appears at the back of a book. It lists all the important topics in alphabetical order. The index and the table of contents can help you find information quickly.

► Use Your Research

You can add the new information gathered from your research to your sequence chart. The writer learned some important things from his research. How did he change his chart?

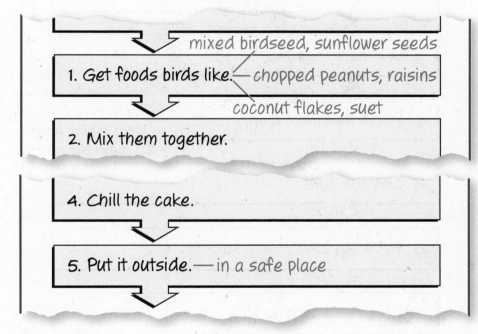

1. Get foods birds like: — mixed birdseed, sunflower seeds
— chopped peanuts, raisins
coconut flakes, suet

2. Mix them together.

4. Chill the cake.

5. Put it outside. — in a safe place

Checklist ✔

Research and Inquiry

- **Did you list your questions?**

- **Did you identify possible resources?**

- **Did you take notes?**

PRACTICE AND APPLY

Review Your Plan

1. Look at your prewriting chart.

2. List questions you have about your topic.

3. Identify the resources that will help you find answers to your questions.

4. Add new information you gather to your chart.

Draft

Writing PROCESS

Before you begin writing your instructions, review the chart you made. Which steps are related? Think about putting related steps in the same paragraph. Include details that describe the steps and support the main idea of each paragraph.

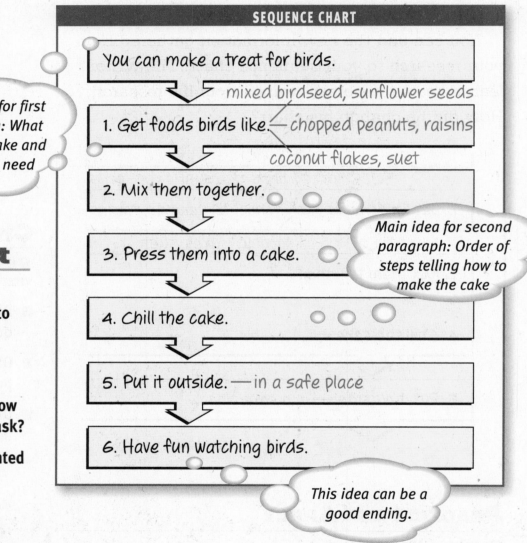

SEQUENCE CHART

You can make a treat for birds.

Main idea for first paragraph: What you can make and what you need

1. Get foods birds like. — mixed birdseed, sunflower seeds / chopped peanuts, raisins / coconut flakes, suet

2. Mix them together.

3. Press them into a cake.

Main idea for second paragraph: Order of steps telling how to make the cake

4. Chill the cake.

5. Put it outside. — in a safe place

6. Have fun watching birds.

This idea can be a good ending.

✓ Checklist

Drafting

■ Does your how-to writing fit your purpose and audience?

■ Have you told how to complete a task?

■ Have you presented step-by-step directions?

■ Did you include details that are easy to follow?

Look at how this writer used the ideas in his chart to write a first draft. He began with a topic sentence that stated the main idea. In the first paragraph, he added details about the foods birds like. In the second paragraph, he wrote the directions in step-by-step order.

PREWRITE

DRAFT

REVISE

PROOFREAD

PUBLISH

DRAFT

You can make a treat to feed birds. First, gather foods that birds like. You can use mixed birdseed. You can use sunflower seeds. Add some chopped peanuts, raisins, or coconut flakes. You also need some suet to hold the foods together.

Put all the ingredients in a bowl and mix them together Press down hard to form a cake. Chill the cake. When the suet cake is firm, remove it from the bowl. Put the birds treet outside where they can reach it safely. Finally, have fun watching the birds enjoy their treat!

Main idea of first paragraph

Details tell what you will need.

Directions are given in step-by-step order.

Last sentence is a good ending.

PRACTICE AND APPLY
Draft Your Own Instructions

1. Review your prewriting chart.
2. Explain how to do or make something.
3. Write directions in step-by-step order.

TECHNOLOGY
Give your document a name that you will remember. You may wish to include the word *draft* in the name.

Revise

Elaborate

When you elaborate, you add ideas and details that make your writing clearer and more interesting. When you revise your instructions, you may wish to add words that explain the meaning of unfamiliar words.

By adding these details, the writer makes the opening sentence livelier.

> *special* *hungry*
> You can make a treat to feed birds.

The writer added words that tell the reader the meaning of the word *suet*.

> Add some chopped peanuts, raisins, or coconut
> *, or hard fat,*
> flakes. You also need some suet to hold the foods
> together.

Word Choice

When you are writing, it is important to choose just the right words for your topic and purpose.

In how-to writing, you need to use words that show the order of the steps to follow. You also need to choose words that describe where things go.

> *Next,*
> Put all the ingredients in a bowl and mix them
> *in the bottom of the bowl*
> together Press down hard to form a cake.

SPACE-ORDER WORDS

top
above
over
middle
halfway
between
bottom
down
below
under
inside
outside
beside

Better Sentences

As you revise your draft, check your sentences to make sure they go together well. Read the sentences aloud. Are they all short? Do they repeat words and sound choppy? If so, you may want to combine two short sentences into one longer sentence.

Sometimes you can combine sentences by joining two nouns.

> You can use mixed birdseed. ~~You can use~~
> and
> sunflower seeds.

PRACTICE AND APPLY

Revise Your Own Instructions

1. Take out information that is not necessary.

2. Add details that will make your writing clearer and more interesting.

3. Add time-order or space-order words.

4. **Grammar** Can you combine any short sentences?

PREWRITE

DRAFT

REVISE

PROOFREAD

PUBLISH

TECHNOLOGY

When you begin revising your draft, you can rename your work using the SAVE AS feature so that you can cut and paste from the original work if you change your mind.

Revise • Peer Conferencing

Share your first draft with a partner. Your partner may have some helpful suggestions.

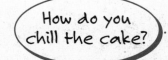

This sounds like fun to do! ....

You can make a treat to feed birds. First, gather foods that birds like. You can use mixed birdseed. You can use sunflower seeds. Add some chopped peanuts, raisins, or coconut flakes. You also need some suet to hold the foods together.

Put all the ingredients in a bowl and mix them together Press down hard to form a cake. Chill the cake. When the suet cake is firm, remove it from the bowl. Put the birds treet outside where they can reach it safely. Finally, have fun watching the birds enjoy their treat!

How do you chill the cake? ....

Where would a safe place be? ....

Good ending! ....

TiP!

Conferencing for the Reader

■ **Does your partner's piece have the features of explanatory writing?**

- • tells how to do or make something
- • step-by-step instructions
- • clear details
- • time-order or space-order words

■ **Be sure to tell your partner what you liked about the piece, as well as ways to improve it.**

As you revise your instructions, think about your partner's comments and suggestions. This writer made some changes based on his partner's ideas.

REVISE

How to make a cake for Birds

You can make a ^special treat to feed ^hungry birds. First,

gather foods that birds like. You can use mixed

birdseed. ~~You can use~~ and sunflower seeds. Add some

chopped peanuts, raisins, or coconut flakes. You

also need some suet , or hard fat, to hold the foods together.

Next, Put all the ingredients in a bowl and mix them

together Press down hard to form a cake in the bottom of the bowl. Chill the

cake in the refrigerator. When the suet cake is firm, remove it from

the bowl. Put the birds treet outside where they

A good place is on top of a pole ⊙ can reach it safely. Finally, have fun watching the

birds enjoy their treat!

PRACTICE AND APPLY

Revise Your Own Instructions

1. Share your draft with a partner and write down your partner's helpful suggestions.

2. Use information from your peer conference to improve your draft.

3. Read your draft aloud and listen to how it sounds.

4. Think of a good title.

Checklist ✔

Revising

■ Do your instructions suit your purpose and audience?

■ Did you write the instructions in step-by-step order? Did you describe each step in detail?

■ Have you included time-order and space-order words?

■ Do you like how your sentences sound?

■ Did you add a good title?

81

Proofread/Edit

After you have revised your how-to writing, you will need to proofread it to find and correct any mistakes in mechanics, grammar and usage, and spelling.

STRATEGIES FOR PROOFREADING

- Reread your revised instructions. Each time, look for a different type of mistake. That way, you'll have a better chance of catching all the mistakes.

- Read the title for correct capitalization of important words.

- Check the ending of each possessive noun.

- Reread for missing end marks.

- Check each word carefully for spelling mistakes.

TiP!

Spelling

When a one-syllable word ends in one vowel followed by one consonant, double the consonant before adding an ending that begins with a vowel. *(chop + ed = chopped)*

REVIEW THE RULES

GRAMMAR

- To form possessive nouns: Add an apostrophe (') and an *s* to a singular noun and to plural nouns that do not end in *s*. Add an apostrophe to most plural nouns that end in *s*.

- You can combine two sentences by joining nouns with the word *and*. Leave out the words that repeat.

MECHANICS

- Each important word in a proper noun and a book title begins with a capital letter.

- An abbreviation begins with a capital letter and ends with a period.

Go to pages 138–165 to review other rules.

Look at the proofreading corrections made on the draft below. What does the proofreading mark ≡ mean? Why does the writer use this mark?

PROOFREAD

How to make a cake for Birds

special   hungry
You can make a treat to feed birds. First,

gather foods that birds like. You can use mixed

and
birdseed. You can use sunflower seeds. Add some

chopped peanuts, raisins, or coconut flakes. You

, or hard fat,
also need some suet to hold the foods together.
Next,
Put all the ingredients in a bowl and mix them
in the bottom of the bowl
together. Press down hard to form a cake. Chill the
in the refrigerator
cake. When the suet cake is firm, remove it from
, treat
the bowl. Put the birds treet outside where they
A good place is on top of a pole .
can reach it safely. Finally, have fun watching the

birds enjoy their treat!

Checklist ✓
Proofreading

■ Do you use capital letters correctly?

■ Did you add the correct ending to possessive nouns?

■ Did you indent each paragraph?

■ Did you spell all the words correctly?

PROOFREADING MARKS

⌗ new paragraph

∧ add

⌇ take out

≡ Make a capital letter.

/ Make a small letter.

(sp) Check the spelling.

⊙ Add a period.

PRACTICE AND APPLY

Proofread Your Own Instructions

1. Correct any mistakes in capitalization.

2. Fix incorrect endings of possessive nouns.

3. Correct spelling mistakes.

4. Indent each paragraph.

Publish

Before you publish, review your instructions one more time. A checklist like the one below can help you.

✓ **Self-Check** Explanatory Writing

❑ **What was my purpose? Did I state it in a topic sentence at the beginning?**

❑ **Who was my audience? Did I use clear details that will help everyone follow my instructions?**

❑ **Did I write the instructions in a step-by-step order?**

❑ **Did I use time-order or space-order words to help the audience understand what to do?**

❑ **Did I use different types of sentences? Do they fit together well?**

❑ **Did I proofread carefully and correct any mistakes?**

The writer used the checklist to review his instructions. Read "How to Make a Cake for Birds" and discuss the published piece. Do you think it was ready to publish? Why do you think so?

How to Make a Cake for Birds

by Jeff Moore

You can make a special treat to feed hungry birds. First, gather foods that birds like. You can use mixed birdseed and sunflower seeds. Add some chopped peanuts, raisins, or coconut flakes. You also need some suet, or hard fat, to hold the foods together.

Next, put all the ingredients in a bowl and mix them together. Press down hard to form a cake in the bottom of the bowl. Chill the cake in the refrigerator.

When the suet cake is firm, remove it from the bowl. Put the birds' treat outside where they can reach it safely. A good place is on top of a pole. Finally, have fun watching the birds enjoy their treat!

PREWRITE

DRAFT

REVISE

PROOFREAD

PUBLISH

TIP!

Handwriting

If you are not writing on a computer, use your neatest handwriting when you publish. Write on one side of the paper only and leave wide margins on all sides.

PRACTICE AND APPLY

Publish Your Own Instructions

1. Give your revised draft one final check.

2. Copy your draft neatly.

3. Add some drawings or photos.

How-to Writing	
Score	**Description**
4 Excellent	■ creates a focused explanation with clear details ■ explains the topic in an engaging manner and logical order ■ uses a personal style and demonstrates original knowledge ■ uses time-order words and precise verbs ■ uses a variety of sentences that flow ■ is free or almost free of errors
3 Good	■ creates a solid explanation with clear details ■ introduces the topic and explanation in a logical order ■ uses a personal tone and shows new knowledge ■ includes some time-order words and precise verbs ■ uses a variety of complete sentences ■ has minor errors that do not confuse the reader
2 Fair	■ tries to explain, but details may be unclear ■ presents some steps or ideas out of order ■ does not connect with readers ■ includes few time-order words and weak verbs ■ uses only simple sentences that lack variety ■ makes frequent errors that confuse the reader
1 Unsatisfactory	■ creates an incomplete explanation ■ does not include a clear beginning or show signs of logical order ■ does not use a personal voice and shows little knowledge of the topic ■ uses words not connected to the purpose ■ uses run-on sentences and sentence fragments ■ makes serious and repeated errors

Go to www.macmillanmh.com for a 6-Point Student Writing Rubric.

Unit 5
Expository Writing: Writing That Compares

Writing That Compares

Sometimes a writer will describe two things by explaining how they are alike and how they are different. This is called writing that compares.

Learning from Writers

Read the following examples of writing that compares. What are the writers describing? As you read, notice how the writers use facts and details to tell how things are alike and how they are different.

THINK AND WRITE

Purpose

How does describing things by comparing them help readers? Write your answer in your journal.

Bigger Than a Dinosaur

The blue whale is the biggest creature that has ever lived on Earth! Female blue whales are a little bigger than the males. Blue whales can grow to 100 feet long and weigh 150 tons—that's heavier than 25 elephants or 115 giraffes.

Reach out and touch the blue whale's skin. It's springy and smooth like a hard-boiled egg, and it's as slippery as wet soap.

Look into its eye. It's as big as a teacup and as dark as the deep sea. Just behind the eye is a hole as small as the end of a pencil. The hole is one of the blue whale's ears—sticking-out ears would get in the way when the whale is swimming.

The blue whale lives all of its long life in the sea. But it is a mammal like us, and it breathes air, not water. From time to time, it has to come to the surface to breathe through the blowholes on top of its head.

—Nicola Davies, from *Big Blue Whale*

Uranus

Uranus is very different from Earth. The planet Earth has one moon, but the planet Uranus has at least 15 moons. Another way Uranus is different is that it has several rings.

Both Uranus and Earth are part of the same solar system, but they move differently. Earth spins like a top. Earth takes one day to rotate once. It takes Earth one year to go around the sun. Uranus, however, rolls on its side like a ball. Unlike Earth, it takes Uranus about 17 hours to rotate once and about 84 years to go around the sun.

Uranus was the first planet to be discovered by a telescope. It has a light blue color. From space, Earth also looks blue.

— Michael Franklin

PRACTICE AND APPLY

Thinking Like a Reader

1. What two facts about the size of a blue whale did you learn from "Bigger Than a Dinosaur"?

2. Name one way Earth and Uranus are alike and one way they are different.

Thinking Like a Writer

3. How did Nicola Davies help you better understand a blue whale's size?

4. How did the writer of "Uranus" organize facts to show how the planets are alike and different?

5. **Reading Across Texts** What words do the writers use to help them compare and contrast two things?

Features of Writing That Compares

DEFINITIONS AND FEATURES

Writing that compares often looks at how things are alike and how they are different. Successful writing that compares:

▸ Explains **how things are alike.**

▸ Explains **how things are different.**

▸ Organizes details in **an order that makes sense.**

▸ Uses **compare and contrast words.**

▸ How Two Things Are Alike

Reread "Bigger Than a Dinosaur" on page 88. What does the author compare a whale's skin to?

Reach out and touch the blue whale's skin. It's springy and smooth like a hard-boiled egg . . .

The author compares the whale's skin to a hard-boiled egg. She explains that these two things are alike because both are springy and smooth.

▸ How Two Things Are Different

The sentence below tells how female blue whales and male blue whales are different. Why do you think the author included this detail?

Female blue whales are a little bigger than the males.

This fact helps the reader understand that the size of blue whales varies. The reader may also find the information interesting and surprising.

▶ An Order That Makes Sense

Presenting details in an order that makes sense helps keep comparisons clear. In the sentences below, the author describes a whale's eye and then a whale's ear.

> Look into its eye. It's as big as a teacup and as dark as the deep sea. Just behind the eye is a hole as small as the end of a pencil. The hole is one of the blue whale's ears. . . .

Why does the order of these details make sense?

▶ Compare and Contrast Words

To help your readers understand how the ideas in your writing are related, you need to use words that will help them compare and contrast two things.

> It's springy and smooth like a hard-boiled egg, and it's as slippery as wet soap.

What words did the author use to compare a whale's skin to a hard-boiled egg and to wet soap?

PRACTICE AND APPLY

Create a Features Chart

1. List the features of writing that compares.

2. Reread "Uranus" by Michael Franklin on page 89.

3. Write one example of each feature in Michael's writing.

4. Write what you liked about Michael's writing.

Features	Examples

Writing PROCESS

Prewrite

Writing that compares often tells how things are alike and how they are different. This kind of writing gives you a chance to write about related ideas.

Purpose and Audience

The purpose of writing that compares is to describe two things. Think about your audience before you begin to write. How will you present your ideas to them?

Choose a Topic

Think about what you would like to compare. If you decide to compare animals, **brainstorm** pairs of animals in one group that are alike in some ways. Choose two animals. Then **explore ideas** for your topic by listing the things you know about the animals.

THiNK AND WRITE

Audience
How will you help your audience understand how the subjects you compare are alike and how they are different? Write your answer.

I explored my ideas by brainstorming.

Coyotes	Wolves
bushy tail	live in different climates
smaller	howl
pointed ears	bigger
live alone	good hunters
howl	bushy tail
good hunters	pointed ears
live in different climates	live in packs

Organize • Sort

When you compare two things, you need to sort the details into two groups. One group of details tells how the two things are alike, and the other group of details tells how they are different. You can use a Venn diagram to organize the details. How did this writer organize the details from her list?

PREWRITE

DRAFT

REVISE

PROOFREAD

PUBLISH

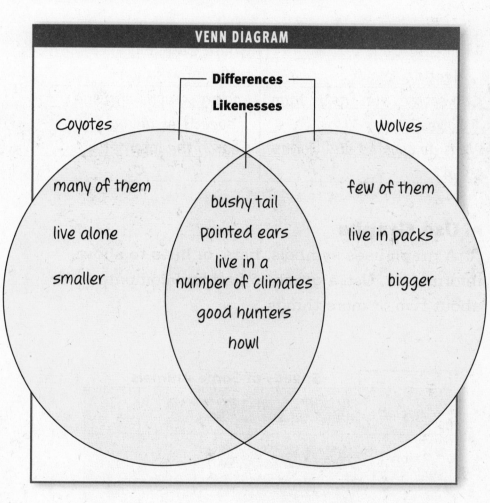

VENN DIAGRAM

Differences

Likenesses

Coyotes

Wolves

many of them

live alone

smaller

bushy tail

pointed ears

live in a number of climates

good hunters

howl

few of them

live in packs

bigger

Checklist ✓
Prewriting

- Have you thought about your purpose and audience?

- Have you chosen two things to compare and explored ideas about them?

- Did you organize details in an order that makes sense?

- Do you need to do any research?

PRACTICE AND APPLY

Plan Your Own Writing That Compares

1. Think about your purpose and audience.

2. Brainstorm ideas for a topic.

3. Choose a topic and explore ideas.

4. Organize your ideas.

Writing PROCESS

Prewrite • Research and Inquiry

▶ Writer's Resources

You may need to do some research to gather information for your writing that compares. Make a list of questions. Then decide what resources you need to find the answers.

What Else Do I Need to Know?	Where Can I Find the Information?
Can coyotes run faster than wolves?	Look at graphs showing speeds of animals.
What do coyotes and wolves eat?	Search the Internet.

▶ Use Graphs

A graph uses symbols, bars, or lines to show information. Use a graph to find and compare facts about two or more things.

This part of the bar graph lists the names of the things being compared.

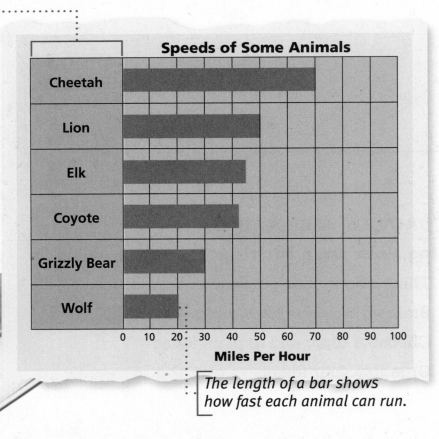

Speeds of Some Animals

	0	10	20	30	40	50	60	70	80	90	100
Cheetah											
Lion											
Elk											
Coyote											
Grizzly Bear											
Wolf											

Miles Per Hour

The length of a bar shows how fast each animal can run.

94

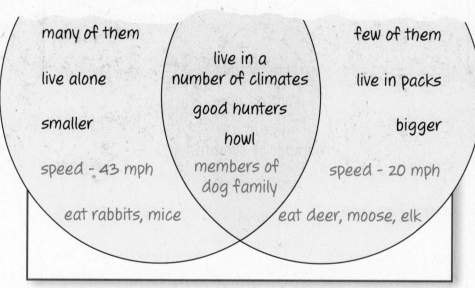

► Search Online

A computer that is connected to the Internet can help you research your topic. Follow instructions to connect to the Internet. Then do a "keyword search" by typing in the name of your subject. The first list you see can point you toward more specific sites on the World Wide Web. Click on the links until you find the information you need for your writing.

Use Your Research

Add the new information from your research to your Venn diagram. What new facts did this writer learn from her research?

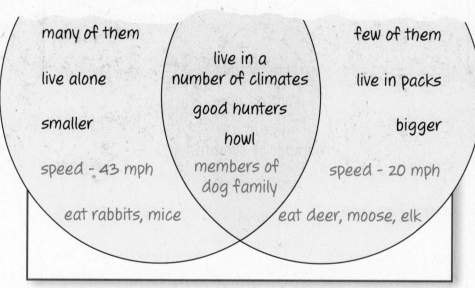

many of them

live alone

smaller

speed - 43 mph

eat rabbits, mice

live in a number of climates

good hunters

howl

members of dog family

few of them

live in packs

bigger

speed - 20 mph

eat deer, moose, elk

Checklist ✓

Research and Inquiry

- ■ Did you write down questions?
- ■ Did you decide what resources to use?
- ■ Did you take notes?

PRACTICE AND APPLY

Review Your Plan

1. Look at your prewriting diagram.

2. List questions you have about your topic.

3. Identify the resources you will need to find answers.

4. Add new information you gather to your diagram.

Draft

Before you begin your writing that compares, review the Venn diagram you made. Think about making a paragraph for likenesses and a paragraph for differences. Include details that support each main idea.

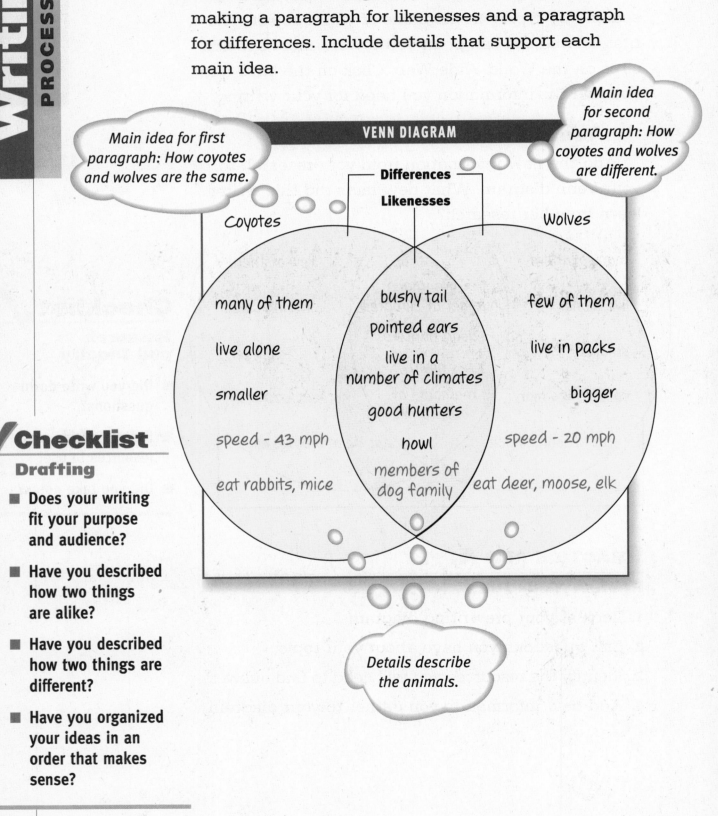

Main idea for first paragraph: How coyotes and wolves are the same.

VENN DIAGRAM

Main idea for second paragraph: How coyotes and wolves are different.

Differences

Likenesses

Coyotes

Wolves

many of them

live alone

smaller

speed - 43 mph

eat rabbits, mice

bushy tail

pointed ears

live in a number of climates

good hunters

howl

members of dog family

few of them

live in packs

bigger

speed - 20 mph

eat deer, moose, elk

Details describe the animals.

✓ Checklist

Drafting

- Does your writing fit your purpose and audience?

- Have you described how two things are alike?

- Have you described how two things are different?

- Have you organized your ideas in an order that makes sense?

Look at how this writer used the information in her diagram to write a first draft. She used details from the middle of the diagram in the first paragraph. She put details from the rest of the diagram in the second paragraph.

PREWRITE

DRAFT

REVISE

PROOFREAD

PUBLISH

DRAFT

Coyotes and wolfs are the same in many ways. ···· Main idea of first paragraph

Coyotes are like wolves because both are wild members of the dog family. Both have pointed ears and a bushy tail. Both can live in different climates, and both are good hunters. Both howl at night. ···· Supporting details tell ways coyotes and wolves are alike.

Coyotes and wolves are different. Coyotes is ···· Main idea of second paragraph

smaller and faster than wolves. Wolves live in packs, but most coyotes live alone. These animals also eat different food. Wolves eat deer moose or elk. Coyotes eat rabbits and mice. Coyotes can run 43 miles per hour, and wolves can run 20 miles per hour. ···· Supporting details tell ways coyotes and wolves are different.

TECHNOLOGY

If you need to change the order of details, you can use the cut and paste feature to move words and sentences.

PRACTICE AND APPLY

Draft Your Own Writing That Compares

1. Review your prewriting diagram.

2. Write paragraphs that describe how two things are alike and how they are different.

3. Give details in an order that makes sense.

Revise

Elaborate

As you work on your draft, you can elaborate. When you elaborate, you add details that help make your writing clearer. When you revise your writing that compares, you may need to add details to help your reader understand the information about the animals.

The writer added words to explain what a pack is.

> *family groups called*
> Wolves live in packs, but most coyotes live alone.

The writer added words to make it clear that the animals that wolves eat are large.

> *large animals, like*
> Wolves eat deer moose or elk.

Word Choice

Good writers think about their topic and audience when they choose words to use.

In writing that compares, you need to find words that will help you compare and contrast two things.

> *In one way,*
> Coyotes are like wolves because both are wild
> *also*
> members of the dog family. Both have pointed
>
> ears and a bushy tail.

COMPARE/ CONTRAST WORDS

alike
same
like
another
also
too
different
and
but
yet
however
although
in one way
in another way
in other ways

Better Paragraphs

Read your paragraphs aloud. Listen to how they sound. Are the paragraphs connected? Do you have a strong closing paragraph?

You may want to add a connecting phrase to help readers move smoothly from one paragraph to the next.

> In other ways,
> ∧Coyotes and wolves are different.

The writer changed this detail to an imaginative closing paragraph.

> In some places, you can hear both animals at
> ~~Both howl at night.~~
> ∧night, howling at the moon.

PRACTICE AND APPLY

Revise Your Own Writing That Compares

1. Add details to help the reader picture what you are describing.

2. Use compare and contrast words.

3. Add words or phrases to connect your paragraphs.

4. Include an interesting closing paragraph.

5. **Grammar** Have you used the correct forms of linking verbs?

TECHNOLOGY

Learn how to use the thesaurus on a computer to replace repeated or general words with more exact or interesting choices.

Revise • Peer Conferencing

Share your writing with a partner. Read your first draft aloud and ask your partner for ideas and suggestions.

Coyotes and wolfs are the same in many ways. Coyotes are like wolves because both are wild members of the dog family. Both have pointed ears and a bushy tail. Both can live in different climates, and both are good hunters. Both howl at night.

Coyotes and wolves are different. Coyotes is smaller and faster than wolves. Wolves live in packs, but most coyotes live alone. These animals also eat different food. Wolves eat deer moose or elk. Coyotes eat rabbits and mice. Coyotes can run 43 miles per hour, and wolves can run 20 miles per hour.

I like these details. They help me picture the animals.

Can you add a compare and contrast word?

These details don't make sense here. You need a better ending.

Conferencing for the Reader

- Did your partner include features of writing that compares? Did he or she
  - explain how two things are alike and different?
  - use details in an order that makes sense?
  - use compare and contrast words?
- Tell your partner what is good about the writing as well as what could be better.

When you revise your writing, think about your partner's ideas. This writer made some changes based on her partner's suggestions.

PREWRITE

DRAFT

REVISE

PROOFREAD

PUBLISH

REVISE

Coyotes and Wolves
^

Coyotes and wolfs are the same in many ways.

In one way,
Coyotes are like wolves because both are wild
^
                                                    also
members of the dog family. Both ˄ have pointed ears

and a bushy tail. Both can live in different climates,

and both are good hunters. ~~Both howl at night.~~

In other ways,
Coyotes and wolves are different. Coyotes is
^
                                          family groups called
smaller and faster than wolves. Wolves live in packs,
                                                ^
but most coyotes live alone. These animals also eat
                                    large animals, like
different food. Wolves eat deer moose or elk.
                              ^
          , however,
Coyotes ˄ eat rabbits and mice. | Coyotes can run 43
        ^
miles per hour, and wolves can run 20 miles per hour. |

In some places, you can hear both animals at night,
howling at the moon

PRACTICE AND APPLY

Revise Your Own Writing That Compares

1. Listen to your draft as you read it aloud to a partner.

2. Write down ideas that your partner suggests.

3. Use the suggestions you like to revise your draft.

4. Add a title.

Checklist ✓

Revising

- Is your writing right for your purpose and audience?

- Do you need to describe anything in more detail?

- Did you use compare and contrast words?

- Did you write your ideas in an order that makes sense?

- Do your sentences and paragraphs blend together for smooth reading?

- Did you add a good title?

Proofread/Edit

Proofread your revised writing to find and correct any mistakes in mechanics, grammar and usage, and spelling.

Writing PROCESS

STRATEGIES FOR PROOFREADING

- **Reread your revised draft.** Each time, look for a different type of mistake.

- **Check for correct spelling.** Use a dictionary.

- **Check for correct punctuation.** Make sure that each sentence has the correct end mark.

- **Check that you used capital letters correctly.**

- **Check for correct forms of linking verbs.** Read aloud to make sure subjects and verbs agree.

Spelling

To make plurals of words that end with one *f* or *fe*, you usually change the *f* to *v* and add *-es* or *-s*. (wolf = wolves)

REVIEW THE RULES

GRAMMAR

- Use the correct form of the linking verb *be*. Use the present-tense form *is* with a singular noun, and *are* with a plural noun. Use the past-tense form *was* with a singular noun, and *were* with a plural noun.

MECHANICS

- Use commas to separate three or more words in a series.

- An apostrophe (') takes the place of letters left out of a contraction.

- An apostrophe is used with nouns to show possession.

Go to pages 138–165 to review other rules.

Look at the proofreading corrections made on the draft below. What does the mark ℒ mean? Why does the writer use this mark?

PROOFREAD

Coyotes and Wolves

wolves
Coyotes and wolfs are the same in many ways.
In one way,
Coyotes are like wolves because both are wild
also
members of the dog family. Both have pointed ears

and a bushy tail. Both can live in different climates,

and both are good hunters. Both howl at night.
In other ways,
are
Coyotes and wolves are different. Coyotes is
family groups called
smaller and faster than wolves. Wolves live in packs,

but most coyotes live alone. These animals also eat

large animals, like
different food. Wolves eat deer, moose, or elk.
, however,
Coyotes eat rabbits and mice. Coyotes can run 43

miles per hour, and wolves can run 20 miles per hour.

In some places, you can hear both animals at night,
howling at the moon.

PRACTICE AND APPLY

Proofread Your Own Writing That Compares

1. Check forms of the linking verb *be*.

2. Add missing punctuation marks.

3. Correct spelling mistakes and indent paragraphs.

Checklist ✓
Proofreading

■ **Did you correct any incorrect forms of the verb *be*?**

■ **Did you end each sentence correctly?**

■ **Did you use an apostrophe to show letters left out of a contraction?**

■ **Did you spell all words correctly?**

■ **Did you indent each paragraph?**

PROOFREADING MARKS

new paragraph

∧ add

ℒ take out

= Make a capital letter.

/ Make a small letter.

(SP) Check spelling.

⊙ Add a period.

103

Publish

Writing PROCESS

Look over your writing one more time before you publish it. Use the checklist below.

✓ Self-Check Writing That Compares

❏ Did I clearly explain how two things are alike and different?

❏ Did I use compare and contrast words?

❏ Did I tell things that will inform and interest my audience?

❏ Did I organize details in a way that makes sense?

❏ Did I use connecting phrases to make my paragraphs flow smoothly?

❏ Did I write a strong closing paragraph?

❏ Did I use correct forms of verbs?

❏ Did I proofread and correct any mistakes?

Before publishing "Coyotes and Wolves," the writer used the checklist to review her writing. Read her writing with a partner and talk about it. Do you think the checklist helped her? What makes you think so?

Coyotes and Wolves

by Emily Wilson

Coyotes and wolves are the same in many ways. In one way, coyotes are like wolves because both are wild members of the dog family. Both also have pointed ears and a bushy tail. Both can live in different climates, and both are good hunters.

In other ways, coyotes and wolves are different. Coyotes are smaller and faster than wolves. Coyotes can run 43 miles per hour, and wolves can run 20 miles per hour. Wolves live in family groups called packs, but most coyotes live alone. These animals also eat different food. Wolves eat large animals, like deer, moose, or elk. Coyotes, however, eat rabbits and mice.

In some places, you can hear both animals at night, howling at the moon.

PREWRITE

DRAFT

REVISE

PROOFREAD

PUBLISH

PRACTICE AND APPLY

Publish Your Own Writing That Compares

1. Check your revised draft one more time.

2. Make a neat final copy.

3. Add a cover and graphs or pictures.

TiP!

Handwriting

Leave a margin on each side of the paper as you write your final copy. Look ahead to the end of each line to see if a word will fit. Do not try to fit a word into a space that is too small.

Writing That Compares

Score	Description
4 Excellent	■ compares and contrasts two items or topics with supporting details ■ arranges ideas logically with good transitions ■ shows detailed knowledge of the subject and conveys that to reader ■ uses precise compare and contrast words ■ uses a variety of sentences that flow ■ is free or almost free of errors
3 Good	■ compares and contrasts two items or topics ■ organizes the comparison well and includes transitions ■ uses an informative tone ■ uses compare and contrast words effectively ■ uses a variety of complete sentences ■ has minor errors that do not confuse the reader
2 Fair	■ makes an unclear comparison with few details ■ does not identify the topic and lacks logical order ■ shows incomplete knowledge and doesn't connect with reader ■ uses few compare and contrast words ■ uses only simple or choppy sentences ■ makes frequent errors that confuse the reader
1 Unsatisfactory	■ does not make a comparison of two items or topics ■ lacks organization or flow ■ shows little or no knowledge and confuses the reader ■ uses only general or vague words ■ uses run-on sentences and sentence fragments ■ makes serious and repeated errors

Go to www.macmillanmh.com for a 6-Point Student Writing Rubric.

Unit 6
Expository Writing: Research Report

Expository Writing: Research Report

Have you ever looked in different books and other sources to find information about a topic? Did you use that information to write a report? A report is expository writing. The purpose of a report is to share information about a topic.

Learning from Writers

Read the following examples of expository writing. What information is included? How is it organized? As you read, notice how each author connects ideas.

THINK AND WRITE

Purpose
How is expository writing different from a personal narrative? Write a short explanation.

Clean as a Breeze

Whirling windmills have been used for energy in countries such as the Netherlands for hundreds of years. Today, windmills are popping up all over the U.S., Europe, and Asia. The modern windmills have lightweight blades that can catch more wind than ever before. They turn the wind into electricity.

One day, we will run out of coal and oil. But we will never run out of the energy we can get from the sun and the wind. Nancy Hazard says, "Energy from the sun and the wind is the key to the future."

— from "Pure Power!" in *Time for Kids*

How Frogs Live on Land and in the Water

Frogs are found in many places. They can live in water, on land, or even in trees. But all frogs start out in the water.

A frog begins as a tadpole that hatches from an egg. It lives underwater and breathes through gills like a fish. As the tadpole turns into a frog, it grows legs and lungs so it can live on land.

Although adult frogs have lungs, they take in most of the oxygen they need through their skin. Their skin can take oxygen from water or air. That is why they can live in water or on land.

—Suki Park

PRACTICE AND APPLY

Thinking Like a Reader

1. What is the main idea of "Clean as a Breeze"?

2. According to "How Frogs Live on Land and in the Water," what do frogs need so they can live on land?

Thinking Like a Writer

3. How did the author of "Clean as a Breeze" support the main idea?

4. What sources might Suki Park have used to find facts about frogs?

5. **Reading Across Texts** Compare how each of the two examples draws a conclusion based on facts.

Features of Expository Writing: Research Report

DEFINITIONS AND FEATURES

Expository writing gives information about a topic. Good expository writing:

▶ Introduces a **main idea** and supports it with details.

▶ **Summarizes information** from different sources.

▶ Uses **connecting words** to go from one idea to the next.

▶ **Draws a conclusion** based on the facts.

▶ Main Idea

Reread "Clean as a Breeze" on page 108. What is the article about?

> Whirling windmills have been used for energy in countries such as the Netherlands for hundreds of years.

The opening sentence tells you that the article will be about using windmills for energy.

▶ Summarizes Information

Good expository writing summarizes information from more than one source.

> Today, windmills are popping up all over the U.S., Europe, and Asia.

What sources might the writer have used for the information summarized in this sentence?

▶ Connecting Words

Words and phrases such as *because*, *as a result*, and *so* help readers connect related ideas in expository writing.

> One day, we will run out of coal and oil. But we will never run out of the energy we can get from the sun and the wind.

What connecting word did the author use?

▶ Draws a Conclusion

The author ends the article with this conclusion about the importance of wind power.

> Nancy Hazard says, "Energy from the sun and the wind is the key to the future."

What facts in the article support this conclusion?

PRACTICE AND APPLY

Create a Features Chart

1. List the features of good expository writing.
2. Reread "How Frogs Live on Land and in the Water" by Suki Park on page 109.
3. Write one example of each feature in Suki's writing.
4. Write what you liked about Suki's report.

Features	Examples

Prewrite

Expository writing presents information about a topic. Writing a report gives you a chance to summarize and share what you have learned.

Purpose and Audience

The purpose for writing a report is to summarize factual information from different sources. It is also to share what you have learned with your audience.

Before you begin to write, think about your audience. Who will be reading your report? Write your report in a way that will interest your readers.

Choose a Topic

Begin by **brainstorming** a list of topics that interest you. Choose something that your readers might like to learn about.

After choosing a topic, **explore ideas** by listing questions that your report will try to answer.

THINK AND WRITE

Audience
Write down what you need to remember about your audience as you plan and write your report.

I explored my ideas by asking questions.

Guinea Pigs
What are they like?
What do they need?
What can you do with them?
Why do people like them?

Organize • Main Idea

Before you write a report, you need to narrow your topic. Your report should focus on just a few main ideas. To plan your report, you can use an outline. How did this writer organize the ideas from his list?

PREWRITE

DRAFT

REVISE

PROOFREAD

PUBLISH

OUTLINE

Topic: Guinea Pigs

I. What are guinea pigs like?

II. What do guinea pigs need?

III. Why do people like guinea pigs?
   A. Guinea pigs are friendly and fun to watch and pet.

   B. They are small and easy to take care of.

PRACTICE AND APPLY

Plan Your Own Report

1. Think about your purpose and audience.

2. Choose a topic.

3. Explore ideas about your topic.

4. Organize your ideas in an outline.

Checklist ✔

Prewriting

- Have you thought about your purpose and audience?

- Have you chosen a topic and explored ideas about it?

- Have you made a list of ideas to include in your report?

- Are your ideas organized in an outline?

- What research do you need to do?

Writing PROCESS

Prewrite • Research and Inquiry

▶ Writer's Resources

When you write a report, you need to do some research to gather information. Make a list of your questions. Then decide what resources you need to answer your questions. Always use more than one resource.

What Else Do I Need to Know?	Where Can I Find the Information?
What do guinea pigs look like?	Use an encyclopedia.
What do guinea pigs eat?	Look in a telephone directory to find pet shops that sell guinea pigs.
Where can you keep them?	
What must the owner do?	

▶ Use an Encyclopedia

An encyclopedia is a good place to begin your research. Search for your topic on an encyclopedia CD-ROM by typing in key words. You will see a list of articles about your subject. Click on the article that you want to read.

Key words the writer typed in.

ENCYCLOPEDIA

Home | Find: Guinea Pig   GO | Help

ARTICLES:

Guinea Pig	GUINEA PIG, a small, gentle animal with short ears, short legs, and no tail.
Rodent	RODENT, an animal that has a pair of big front teeth used for gnawing.
Mammal	MAMMAL, a kind of animal that is warm-blooded and has a backbone.

▶ Use a Telephone Directory

A telephone directory gives the names, addresses, and phone numbers of people, businesses, and other resources. It is arranged in alphabetical order. You can find extra information about businesses in a section called The Yellow Pages.

▶ Use Your Research

Information gathered from your research goes into your outline. This writer added facts from his research. How did he change the outline?

I. What are guinea pigs like?
   A. many colors of fur; thick bodies, short legs

   B. make lots of noises, chew things

II. What do guinea pigs need?
   A. cage to live in

   B. vegetables and fruit; dry food; fresh water

   C. The owner must clean the cage and feed
      the guinea pig.

Checklist ✔

Research and Inquiry

■ Did you list your questions?

■ Did you identify more than one resource?

■ Did you take notes?

PRACTICE AND APPLY

Review Your Plan

1. Look at your outline.

2. List questions you have about your topic.

3. Identify the resources you need to find answers.

4. Add the information you gather to your outline.

Draft

Before you begin writing your report, review the outline you made. Think about making a paragraph for each main idea. Include details that support each main idea.

Main idea for first paragraph: What guinea pigs are like

Writing PROCESS

Supporting details for first main idea.

✓ Checklist

Drafting

- Does your report suit your purpose and audience?

- Have you given details to support your ideas?

- Have you summarized facts from more than one source?

- Have you drawn a conclusion based on the facts?

OUTLINE

Topic: Guinea Pigs

I. What are guinea pigs like?
  A. many colors of fur; thick bodies, short legs

  B. make lots of noises, chew things

II. What do guinea pigs need?
  A. cage to live in

  B. vegetables and fruit; dry food; fresh water

  C. The owner must clean the cage and feed the guinea pig.

III. Why do people like guinea pigs?
  A. Guinea pigs are friendly and fun to watch and pet.
  B. They are small and easy to take care of.

Look at how this writer used the ideas in his outline to write a first draft. He described guinea pigs in the first paragraph. He told about what they need in the second paragraph. In the third paragraph, he drew a conclusion based on the facts.

PREWRITE

DRAFT

REVISE

PROOFREAD

PUBLISH

DRAFT

Guinea pigs are small, furry animals that come in many different colors. Guinea pigs have thick bodys and short legs. I think they're really cute. Guinea pigs can make a lot of noise.

Main idea of first paragraph

Supporting details further describe guinea pigs.

A pet guinea pig needs a cage to live in. It needs a food dish, a water bottle, and things to chew. guinea pigs need to eat fresh fruits or vegetables every day. It needs fresh water and dry food, too. The cage needs to be cleaned every week.

Main idea of second paragraph

Supporting details explain what guinea pigs need.

Conclusion

Guinea pigs are friendly and their not hard to take care of. Do you like feeding and petting small animals a guinea pig may be the pet for you!

PRACTICE AND APPLY

Draft Your Own Report

1. Review your prewriting outline.

2. Summarize information from your research.

3. Draw a conclusion based on the facts.

TECHNOLOGY

Give your draft a name and a number. After you revise it, do a "save as" with the same name but a different number.

Revise

Elaborate

Reread your first draft. Are any important ideas or details missing? When you revise your report, you may need to elaborate by adding more details.

The details that the writer added tell the reader more about what this pet is like.

> They squeak, squeal, whistle, and purr.
> Guinea pigs can make a lot of noise.∧

The writer added another detail to make this part more complete. When writing a report, you may need to learn new words that are special for your subject.

> or hutch
> A pet guinea pig needs a cage to live in.
>   ∧

Word Choice

When you write, it is important to choose your words carefully so that the reader will know exactly what you mean.

In a report, you need to find words that connect one idea to another.

> Even though they are little,
> ∧Guinea pigs can make a lot of noise.

CONNECTING WORDS

but
so
at first
later
earlier
however
if so
even though
because of
since
as a result
also

Better Sentences

As you are revising your draft, check your sentences to make sure they fit together well. Read your sentences aloud. How do they sound? Have you tried not to begin every sentence with the same subject?

You can use a pronoun to avoid repeating the same noun again and again.

> Guinea pigs are small, furry animals that come in many different colors. ~~Guinea pigs~~ They have thick bodies and short legs.

PRACTICE AND APPLY

Revise Your Own Report

1. Add details that will make your writing clearer and more interesting.

2. Use connecting words to lead your readers from one idea to the next.

3. Take out information that does not support your main ideas.

4. **Grammar** Should you use pronouns in place of some of the nouns in your report?

TECHNOLOGY

Some of your classmates may know word-processing tips or shortcuts. Ask them to share what they know.

119

Revise • Peer Conferencing

Exchange reports with a partner and read each other's first drafts. You may both be able to give each other some fresh ideas and suggestions.

Writing **PROCESS**

Your topic interests me.

Guinea pigs are small, furry animals that come in many different colors. Guinea pigs have thick bodies and short legs. I think they're really cute. Guinea pigs can make a lot of noise.

Your opinion doesn't belong in a report.

A pet guinea pig needs a cage to live in. It needs a food dish, a water bottle, and things to chew. guinea pigs need to eat fresh fruits or vegetables every day. It needs fresh water and dry food, too. The cage needs to be cleaned every week.

These details clearly tell me what it's like to take care of a guinea pig!

Guinea pigs are friendly and their not hard to take care of. Do you like feeding and petting small animals a guinea pig may be the pet for you!

TiP!

Conferencing for the Reader

- Did your partner include features of a report?
  - main idea and supporting details
  - summarizes information
  - connecting words
  - draws a conclusion
- Tell your partner what you like about the report, as well as what could be better.

Think about the comments and suggestions of your partner when you revise your report. This writer made some changes based on his partner's ideas.

REVISE

Guinea Pigs
^

Guinea pigs are small, furry animals that

come in many different colors. ~~Guinea pigs~~ They ꝺ

have thick bodies and short legs. ~~I think they're~~ ꝺ

~~really cute.~~ ꝺ Even though they are little, Guinea pigs can make a lot
^

of noise. They squeak, squeal, whistle, and purr.
^

or hutch   also
A pet guinea pig needs a cage to live in. It
^   ^

needs a food dish, a water bottle, and things to

chew. guinea pigs need to eat fresh fruits or

vegetables every day. It needs fresh water and dry

food, too. The cage needs to be cleaned every week.

Guinea pigs are friendly and their not hard to

take care of. Do you like feeding and petting small
? If so,
animals a guinea pig may be the pet for you!
^

PRACTICE AND APPLY

Revise Your Own Report

1. Have a partner read your report.

2. Take notes on your partner's comments.

3. Use your notes to improve your draft.

4. Add a title.

Checklist ✓
Revising

■ Does your report suit your purpose and audience?

■ Did you include enough details to support your main ideas? Did you choose words carefully?

■ Do the sentences flow smoothly?

■ Did you draw a conclusion based on the facts?

121

Proofread/Edit

Proofread your revised report to find and correct any mistakes in grammar and usage, mechanics, and spelling.

STRATEGIES FOR PROOFREADING

- Reread your revised report, each time looking for a different type of error. **That way you will have a better chance of catching all mistakes.**

- Read each sentence for correct capitalization.

- Reread each sentence for correct punctuation.

- Reread for correct use of possessive pronouns and contractions.

- Check each word for spelling mistakes.

TiP!

Spelling

When a base word ends with a consonant followed by *y*, change the *y* to *i* when adding *-es*. (body = bodies)

REVIEW THE RULES

GRAMMAR

- A pronoun must match the noun it replaces. Use singular pronouns for singular nouns and plural pronouns for plural nouns.

MECHANICS

- Capitalize *I*.

- Refer to yourself last when writing about yourself and someone else.

- A contraction has an apostrophe (') to show missing letters.

- A possessive pronoun does not have an apostrophe.

Go to pages 138–165 to review other rules.

Writing PROCESS

Look at the proofreading corrections made on the draft below. What does the proofreading mark ∧ mean? Why does the writer use this mark?

PROOFREAD

Guinea Pigs
∧

Guinea pigs are small, furry animals that

come in many different colors. ~~Guinea pigs~~ *They* ∿
∧

have thick ~~bodys~~ *bodies* ∿ and short legs. ~~I think they're~~ ∿
∧

~~really cute.~~ *Even though they are little,* Guinea pigs can make a lot
∧

of noise. *They squeak, squeal, whistle, and purr.*
∧

A pet guinea pig needs a cage *or hutch* to live in. It *also*
∧   ∧

needs a food dish, a water bottle, and things to

chew. guinea pigs need to eat fresh fruits or
‗

vegetables every day. ~~It~~ *They* ∿ needs fresh water and dry
∿

food, too. The cage needs to be cleaned every week.

Guinea pigs are friendly, and ~~their~~ *they're* ∿ not hard to
∧

take care of. Do you like feeding and petting small

? If so,
animals ∧ a guinea pig may be the pet for you!
∧

Checklist ✓
Proofreading

- Did you spell all the words correctly?

- Did you begin and end every sentence correctly?

- Does each pronoun match the noun it replaces?

- Are contractions and possessive pronouns written correctly?

PROOFREADING MARKS

⌗ new paragraph

∧ add

∿ take out

‗ Make a capital letter.

／ Make a small letter.

ⓈⓅ Check the spelling.

⊙ Add a period.

PRACTICE AND APPLY

Proofread Your Own Report

1. Correct spelling mistakes and punctuation.

2. Use the correct pronoun.

3. Make sure contractions and possessive pronouns are written correctly.

Publish

Review your report one more time before you publish it. Using a checklist will help you focus.

✓ Self-Check · Expository Writing

❑ **Who is my audience? Did I write in a way that will interest them?**

❑ **What is my purpose? Will the reader learn new facts about the subject?**

❑ **Did I narrow my topic?**

❑ **Did I use information from more than one source?**

❑ **Did I draw a conclusion based on the facts?**

❑ **Did I use pronouns in place of repeated nouns?**

❑ **Did I make sure that all pronouns matched the nouns they replaced?**

❑ **Did I write possessive pronouns correctly?**

The writer used the checklist to review his report. Read "Guinea Pigs" and discuss it with your classmates. Was the piece ready to be published? Why or why not?

Writing PROCESS

Guinea Pigs

by Raphael Garcia

Guinea pigs are small, furry animals that come in many different colors. They have thick bodies and short legs. Even though they are little, guinea pigs can make a lot of noise. They squeak, squeal, whistle, and purr.

A pet guinea pig needs a cage or hutch to live in. It also needs a food dish, a water bottle, and things to chew. Guinea pigs need to eat fresh fruits or vegetables every day. They need fresh water and dry food, too. The cage needs to be cleaned every week.

Guinea pigs are friendly, and they're not hard to take care of. Do you like feeding and petting small animals? If so, a guinea pig may be the pet for you!

TIP!

TECHNOLOGY

For your final report, choose a font size that is easy to read. Adjust your margins to make room for any drawings or photos you plan to use.

PRACTICE AND APPLY

Publish Your Own Report

1. Check your revised draft one more time.
2. Make a neat final copy.
3. Add some drawings or photographs.

Research Report

Score	Description
4 Excellent	■ uses well-researched details that support a main idea ■ includes a strong introduction and conclusion ■ shows deep knowledge of topic and interests reader ■ uses transition words and accurate vocabulary ■ uses a variety of sentences that flow and guide reader ■ is free or almost free of errors
3 Good	■ supports a main idea with solid research ■ has a logical flow of supporting facts and details ■ shows knowledge of the topic in a personal tone ■ uses relevant language and transition words ■ uses a variety of complete sentences ■ has minor errors that do not confuse the reader
2 Fair	■ presents limited research and has no main idea ■ has a weak introduction and conclusion ■ does not fully engage the topic and lacks a personal view ■ chooses weak words for topic with few transition words ■ uses only simple or choppy sentences ■ makes frequent errors that confuse the reader
1 Unsatisfactory	■ does not include research or provide facts about the topic ■ lacks a main idea or organizing structure ■ shows little understanding of topic and no personal style ■ relies on basic vocabulary with no transition words ■ uses run-on sentences and sentence fragments ■ makes serious and repeated errors

Go to www.macmillanmh.com for a 6-Point Student Writing Rubric.

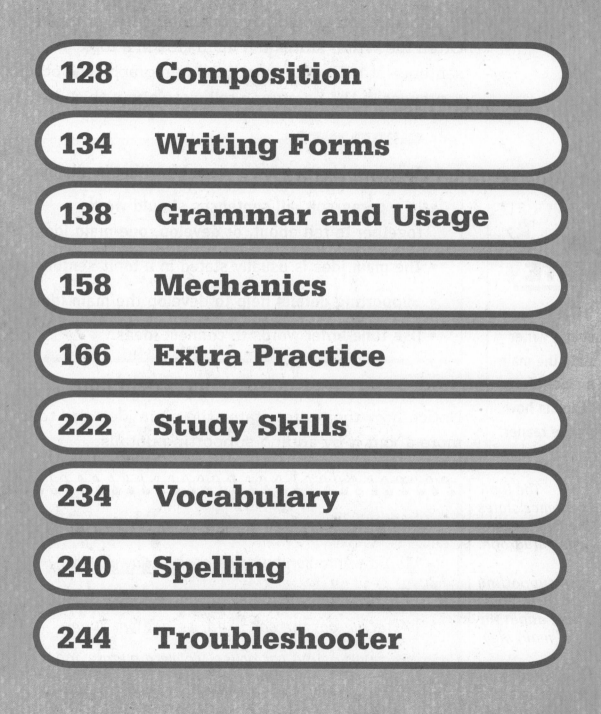

Main Idea and Supporting Details

A paragraph should have one main idea, or topic. Often the writer states the main idea in a topic sentence at the beginning of the paragraph. The other sentences in the paragraph tell more about this idea.

GUIDELINES

- The **main idea** is what a piece of writing is all about.

- In a **paragraph**, all sentences should work together to tell about, or develop, one main idea.

- The main idea is usually stated in a **topic sentence**.

- **Supporting details** help to develop the main idea.

- Use **time-order words** to connect ideas.

Read this paragraph about a personal experience. Notice how the writer states the main idea and tells more about it by adding supporting details.

THINK AND WRITE

Main Idea
Why should a writer clearly state the main idea in a piece of writing? Explain how this helps the reader.

The topic sentence states the main idea of this paragraph.

A supporting detail tells more about the main idea.

A time-order word connects one idea to another.

I'll never forget the day my family moved to San Antonio. It was a very hot day in July. Before we got to the city, our car broke down. After we got the car fixed, we got lost. When we finally found our house, we were hungry and tired. Luckily, our new neighbors were very friendly. They invited us over for supper. Our very bad day had a very good ending. Now that we are settled, we love it here.

Organization

To help the reader follow ideas, events, or instructions, a writer presents ideas and details in an order that makes sense.

GUIDELINES

- **Begin with a topic sentence that states the main idea.**

- **When you explain how to do something, organize the details in the order in which the instructions need to be carried out.**

- **Write exact, step-by-step details.**

THINK AND WRITE

Organization
How can you organize step-by-step details to make your instructions easy to understand? Write your answer.

Read these instructions. Notice how the writer organizes ideas.

You can make a scope to spy on underwater life. First, cut the top and bottom off a large milk carton. Next, cover the bottom and sides with thick, clear plastic. Hold the plastic to the carton with a rubber band. Then tape the plastic to the inside of the open end. After you put your scope together, take it to a pond or stream. Hold the plastic-covered end in the water. Then look down into the scope. Finally, watch the underwater action!

A topic sentence tells what the paragraph is about.

Details tell exactly what to do and are given in step-by-step order.

Time-order words show the order of the steps.

Leads and Endings

Writers use a strong beginning, or lead, to get the reader's attention. They use a good ending to help readers feel that the piece of writing is complete.

GUIDELINES

- The **lead** is the opening of a piece of writing and should grab the reader's attention.

- The lead may give the main idea.

- The **ending** is the last part of a piece of writing and should help readers feel the writing is complete.

- The ending may draw a conclusion, restate the main idea, or sum up what the writer said.

THiNK AND WRITE

Leads and Endings

Why is a strong lead and a good ending important to a piece of writing? Write your answer.

Read this letter. Notice how the writer begins and ends the invitation.

A good lead draws the reader in.

A good ending helps the reader feel the writing is complete.

Dear Aunt Betty,

Have you ever been to Seal Point? Please spend August 4 with us. We'll have a picnic at Seal Point. We can watch the seals and fly kites. If it rains, we'll go to the new science museum. Please come. We'd like to help you celebrate your birthday.

Love,

Liz

Writing Descriptions

A writer uses description to paint a clear and colorful picture for the reader.

GUIDELINES

- A **description** can be about persons, places, or things.

- Each paragraph of a description has a **main-idea sentence** that tells what the paragraph is about.

- Use **sensory details** to describe how things look, sound, smell, taste, and feel.

- Use **likenesses and differences** to order details in writing that compares.

Read the following paragraphs. Notice how the writer uses sensory words to describe how butterflies and moths are alike.

THINK AND WRITE

Writing Descriptions

How can a writer paint a picture with words? Write a brief explanation.

There are several ways that butterflies and moths are alike. Both are insects, and most have four wings. They both have colored scales over their delicate wings. Butterflies, like moths, live in all parts of North America. Some live in wet climates. Others live in dry places. Each likes to sip sweet nectar from flowers.

Butterflies and moths are different in many ways. Butterflies fly in the day, while moths fly at night. Unlike butterflies, moths like bright lights.

A main-idea sentence for the first paragraph

Sensory words paint a picture for the reader.

Details describing differences are in another paragraph.

131

Outlining

Outlining is a good way to organize your ideas for writing. An outline lists main ideas and supporting details for one topic.

GUIDELINES

- An **outline** is a way of organizing ideas.

- Write the **topic** at the top of the outline.

- List the **main ideas** you plan to include. Number each main idea with a Roman numeral, followed by a period.

- Under each main idea, list **supporting details** that help to develop that idea. Give each detail a letter.

- Ideas written in an outline do not need to be complete sentences. They can be words, phrases, or questions.

Read this outline for the first two paragraphs of a report about giraffes. Notice how the writer organizes the main idea and supporting details.

THINK AND WRITE

Outlining

How can an outline help you plan your writing? Write your answer in your journal.

The main idea of the first paragraph is written next to the Roman numeral I.

Each supporting detail for that idea is indented and labeled.

Topic: Giraffes

I. Body features

    A. Long neck

    B. Patchy coat

    C. Knobby forehead

II. Places they live

    A. African grasslands

    B. Wildlife parks, zoos

Beginning, Middle, End

All good writing has a beginning, a middle, and an end. The beginning of a story tells what it will be about. The middle of a story tells what happens. The end of a story tells how everything turns out.

GUIDELINES

- The **beginning** of a story tells who the story is about and when and where the story takes place.

- The **middle** develops the story events, actions, and problems.

- The **end** tells how everything turns out in a way that makes sense.

Read this story. Notice how the writer develops the beginning, the middle, and the end.

THINK AND WRITE

Beginning, Middle, and End
Why is it important for a story to have a clear beginning, middle, and end? Write your answer.

Pecos Bill, old cowhands say, invented roping. He had a rope that stretched across the state of Texas. That rope got him into tons of trouble.

Pecos Bill roped everything he saw. The first time he saw a train, he thought it was a strange animal. He threw his rope over it and hauled it in!

Pecos Bill got quite a surprise when the conductor yelled out, "This is a train, not a cow!" From that day on, Pecos Bill only roped cattle.

An interesting beginning grabs the reader's attention.

The middle of the story tells a clear sequence of events.

A good ending gives readers a feeling of completeness.

Poem

A **poem** is a special kind of writing that uses word pictures to explain, describe, or tell a story. Poems often use rhyme, rhythm, and the sounds of words to "paint a picture" of an idea or a subject.

In poetry, a group of lines is called a stanza. This poem has three stanzas.

This line helps readers picture what a rider on a merry-go-round hears and feels.

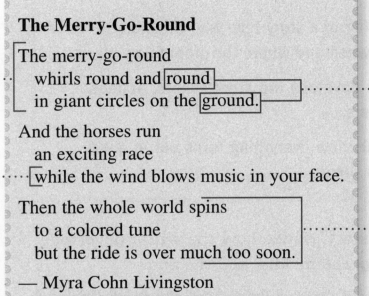

The Merry-Go-Round

The merry-go-round
    whirls round and round
    in giant circles on the ground.

And the horses run
    an exciting race
    while the wind blows music in your face.

Then the whole world spins
    to a colored tune
    but the ride is over much too soon.

— Myra Cohn Livingston

Poetry often rhymes. In this poem, the second and third lines in each stanza end with the same sound.

Poetry often has a rhythm. Read aloud to hear the sound pattern in a poem.

GUIDELINES FOR WRITING A POEM

- **Choose something fun or interesting to write about.**

- **You might choose to capture a special moment or feeling.**

- **Think about the pictures you want to create with words. Decide if you want to use rhyme, rhythm, and the sounds of words.**

- **Write as many stanzas and lines as you want.**

- **Give your poem a title.**

Practice Pretend that you have been named the official town poet. Write and illustrate a poem about what is best about your town.

134

Business Letter

A **business letter** is a formal letter that is written to a person or a company. You can write a business letter to persuade or to inform. You can also write one to ask for something or to apply for a job.

*The **heading** gives the writer's address and the date.*

322 Washington Street
El Paso, Texas 79905
May 12, 20__

*The **inside address** gives the name and address of the person to whom you are writing.*

Mr. James Green
Young Writer's Magazine
1200 South Street
El Paso, Texas 79901

*The **greeting** begins with the word Dear. Use a colon after the name.*

Dear Mr. Green:

*The **body** of the letter tells what you want to say.*

I would like to join the Young Writer's Club that you described in your magazine. I am nine years old, and I love to write. I write articles for the school newspaper. I also enjoy writing poetry.

Please enter me in your club. I understand that there is no charge. I also understand that I will get monthly newsletters that tell about writing contests and new authors. Thank you.

*The **closing** is a way of saying goodbye. Use a capital letter for the first word only. Use a comma after the closing.*

Yours truly,

Sam Jefferson

Sam Jefferson

*The **signature** is the signed name of the writer.*

Practice Write a business letter to one of your favorite authors. Tell the author what you like about his or her writing. Ask one or two questions.

Writing

Play

A **play** is a story that is written to be acted out on a stage for an audience. In a play, characters use words (called dialogue) and actions to tell the story.

A play has a cast of characters.

The setting is when and where the play happens.

An act is one part of a play. Many plays have more than one act.

Stage directions at the beginning of an act tell about the action.

The dialogue is written after each character's name.

Stage directions in ( ) tell how characters speak and act.

The Elves and the Shoemaker

Characters: Shoemaker
Shoemaker's Wife
Elf 1
Elf 2

Setting: Long ago in the shop of a poor shoemaker.

Act One

As the curtain rises, the shoemaker is at his bench. He is speaking to his wife.

Shoemaker (shaking his head) I have enough leather for only one pair of shoes. What are we going to do?

Shoemaker's Wife It's late. Go to bed now. We will worry about money tomorrow.

Shoemaker I'm so tired. If only I had someone who could help me.

Shoemaker's Wife We can't afford to hire anyone.

Shoemaker You go on to bed, dear. I'm going to stay up and work. (The wife goes offstage.) I'm so tired. I can't keep my eyes open. I . . . (The shoemaker falls asleep. Suddenly, the light in the fireplace begins to grow. Elf 1 steps out of the fireplace, turns and whistles. Elf 2 tumbles out of the fireplace. The elves carefully walk over to the Shoemaker and check to make sure he is still asleep.)

Practice Write the first act of a play. You can base your play on a favorite story or folktale.

Writing 6

Editorial

An **editorial** is a newspaper article. It gives the writer's opinion of an event, a situation, or a problem. Editorials appear on the editorial page of a newspaper.

The title of an editorial is called a headline.

The subject of this editorial is a current situation at school.

The writer gives reasons why she thinks her opinion is correct.

A Soccer Field for Our School

Why doesn't our school have a soccer field? I think we need one. We have a nice playing field for baseball. We even have a track for running. But no one has built a field for soccer. If our school had a soccer field, we could start a school soccer team. Also, people in our town could use the field for soccer games on the weekend. There is room behind the cafeteria for a field.

Why don't we build one soon?

Jennifer Felner

The writer states her opinion.

The writer uses facts to persuade readers.

The writer's name is given at the end of the editorial.

GUIDELINES FOR WRITING AN EDITORIAL

- Choose a subject that is important to you.
- Give your opinion and reasons for your opinion.
- Use facts to help persuade your readers.
- Write a title that could be used in the newspaper as a headline.

Practice Write an editorial for your school, town, or city newspaper. Think of an event, a situation, or a problem. Write about your opinion or what you think needs to be changed.

Grammar

Sentences

- A **sentence** is a group of words that expresses a complete thought. It begins with a capital letter.

    Tomas has an interesting hobby.

- A **sentence fragment** is a group of words that does not express a complete thought.

    Collects rocks. (needs a subject)
    One large gray rock. (needs a predicate)

Practice **Write each group of words that is a sentence.**

1. Looks through the rock pile.
2. Tomas sorts the rocks into boxes.
3. Some people collect rocks.
4. Labels each rock.
5. Many museums have rock collections.

Types of Sentences

- When you write or talk, you use different kinds of sentences.

Type of Sentence	Example
A **statement** tells something. It ends with a period.	*You can grow plants in a window box.*
A **question** asks something. It ends with a question mark.	*Should I water the plants every day?*
A **command** tells someone to do something. It ends with a period.	*Don't give the plants too much water.*
An **exclamation** shows strong feeling. It ends with an exclamation mark.	*What a lot of work a garden is!*

Grammar

Practice Write the sentences. Then write *statement, question, command,* or *exclamation* to tell what type of sentence each is.

1. Plant some peppers in the garden.

2. Where can we get seeds?

3. I'll order seeds from this catalog.

4. Don't plant the seeds too close together.

5. What a great garden we'll have!

RULE 3

Subjects in Sentences

- Every sentence has two parts. The subject of a sentence tells what or whom the sentence is about. The subject of a sentence can be more than one word.

    Seeds travel in different ways.
    Dandelion seeds are carried by the wind.

Practice Write the sentences. Draw a line under the subject of each sentence.

1. Some plants have seeds with little hooks.

2. The hooks cling to an animal's fur.

3. The animal carries the seeds to another place.

4. Birds eat fruit and drop the seeds.

5. These seeds grow into plants.

Grammar

RULE 4 — **Predicates in Sentences**

- Every sentence has a subject and a predicate. The predicate tells what the subject does or is.

  Ralph Samuelson invented water skis.
  Ralph was eighteen years old.

Practice **Write the sentences. Draw a line under the predicate of each sentence.**

1. Ralph worked with snow skis.
2. The skis were too narrow.
3. The young inventor made wide skis from boards.
4. A fast boat pulled Ralph across the water.
5. Crowds cheered at the sight.

RULE 5 **Combining Sentences**

- Two sentences with similar ideas can be combined using a comma and the word *and*. This kind of sentence is called a compound sentence.

  It is a clear night, and the stars are bright.

Practice **Write each pair of sentences as one sentence. Use a comma before *and* when you join the sentences.**

1. The earth turns. Stars rise and set like the sun.
2. The teacher sets up a telescope. Students aim it at the stars.
3. Everyone looks closely. Doug finds the North Star first.
4. The moon glows. The stars shine.
5. Amber found a special star. She made a wish.

QUICK WRITE Write one example for each type of sentence.

Grammar

RULE 1 — **Nouns, Singular and Plural**

- A noun names a person, place, or thing.

- A singular noun names one person, place, or thing.
  A plural noun names more than one.

- Add -s to form the plural of most singular nouns.

- Add -es to form the plural of singular nouns that end
  in s, sh, ch, or x.

- To form the plural of nouns ending in a consonant and
  y, change the y to i and add -es.

  cow cows   bush bushes   party parties

Practice Write the sentences. Use the plural form of the
noun in ( ).

1. Many (family) visit Florida in the winter.

2. The weather is warm in most (month).

3. Florida has beautiful (beach).

RULE 2 — **More Plural Nouns**

- Some nouns have special plural forms.

  Those men fed three geese.

- A few nouns have the same singular and plural forms.

  Many moose and deer live in the woods.

Practice Write the sentences. Use the plural form of the
noun in ( ).

1. Those two (woman) are dentists.

2. The dentists take care of people's (tooth).

3. One girl plays with two stuffed (sheep).

Grammar

RULE 3 — **Common and Proper Nouns**

- A **common noun** names any person, place, or thing.

    The girl went to the zoo.

- A **proper noun** names a special person, place, or thing. A proper noun begins with a capital letter.

    Ellen went to the Bronx Zoo.

Practice Write the sentences. Write *common* or *proper* under each underlined noun.

1. The London Zoo had an elephant named Jumbo.
2. The giant animal came from Africa.
3. P. T. Barnum bought the huge beast.
4. The man brought the elephant to the United States.
5. Jumbo amazed people in New York.

RULE 4 — **Singular and Plural Possessive Nouns**

- A **possessive noun** is a noun that shows who or what owns or has something. Add an apostrophe (') and an *s* to a singular noun to make it possessive.

    Dan's friend Edna likes apples.

- Add an apostrophe (') to make most plural nouns possessive.

    Those trees' apples are ripe.

- Add an apostrophe (') and an *s* to form the possessive of plural nouns that do not end in *-s*.

    The children's baskets are full.

Grammar

Practice Write the sentences. Use the possessive form of the noun in ( ).

1. Apple trees grow on (Dan) farm.

2. Apple (growers) work is hard.

3. The (men) job is to pick apples.

4. Apples are many (people) favorite fruit.

5. (Edna) favorite apples are green.

RULE 5

Combining Sentences: Nouns

• Two sentences can be combined by joining two nouns with *and*. Leave out the words that repeat.

Guy wanted a tree house. Pete wanted a tree house.
Guy and Pete wanted a tree house.

Practice Write each pair of sentences as one sentence. Use the word *and* to join two nouns.

1. Guy looked for some wood. Pete looked for some wood.

2. Guy brought a hammer. Guy brought nails.

3. Pete found a ladder. Pete found rope.

4. Guy climbed an old maple tree. Pete climbed an old maple tree.

5. The boys' mother helped. The boys' father helped.

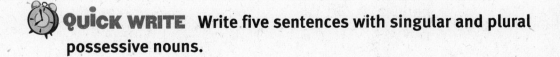 **QUICK WRITE** Write five sentences with singular and plural possessive nouns.

143

RULE 1

Action Verbs

- An **action verb** is a word that shows action.

  Ray climbs the ladder.

- Some action verbs tell about actions that are hard to see.

  Ray thinks about the work.

Practice **Write each sentence. Draw a line under the action verb.**

1. Ray and his friends paint houses.

2. The painters wear white coveralls.

3. Brett stirs a can of paint.

4. Marjorie cleans her brush.

5. Ray brushes paint on the wall.

RULE 2

Linking Verbs

- An **action verb** is a verb that shows action. A **linking verb** does not show action. It connects the subject to the rest of the sentence. The verb *be* is a common linking verb. It has special forms in the present tense and in the past tense.

  Present-tense forms of *be*: *are, is, am*
  Past-tense forms of *be*: *were, was*

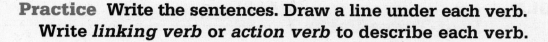
Practice Write the sentences. Draw a line under each verb. Write *linking verb* or *action verb* to describe each verb.

1. The school bus was late.

2. We worried about the bus.

3. The bus driver is sorry.

4. An accident caused a traffic jam.

5. Now I am late for school.

RULE 3 — **Present-Tense Verbs**

- The **tense** of a verb tells when the action takes place.

- A verb in the **present tense** tells what happens now.

   Gary collects seashells.

- When the subject is not *I* or *you*, add *-s* to most singular verbs in the present tense.

- Add *-es* to verbs that end in *sh, ch, ss, s, zz,* or *x*.

- Change *y* to *i* and add *-es* to verbs that end with a consonant and y.

   looks   fixes   worries

Practice Write each sentence. Use the correct form of the verb in ( ).

1. Gary (walk) along the beach.

2. The boy (search) for shells.

3. A big wave (wash) some shells onto the sand.

4. Gary (hurry) to find more shells.

5. The boy (drop) one shell.

Grammar

RULE 4 — Past-Tense Verbs

- A past-tense verb tells about an action that has already happened. Add -ed to most verbs to form the past tense.

  Last night, it snowed.

- Change the *y* to *i* before adding -ed if the verb ends with a consonant and *y*.

- Drop the *e* and add -ed to verbs that end with *e*.

- Double the consonant and add -ed to verbs that end with one vowel and one consonant.

  tried   smiled   planned

Practice Write the sentences. Use the past tense of the verb in ( ).

1. In the morning, snow (cover) the ground.
2. The weather (surprise) us.
3. No one (expect) snow in October!
4. Les and I (grin) at each other.
5. We (bundle) ourselves in warm clothes.
6. Then we (hurry) outside.
7. Les and I (pile) snow into a big mound.
8. We (pack) the snow into a fort.

RULE 5 — Future-Tense Verbs

- A future-tense verb tells about an action that is going to happen. Use the special verb *will* to write about the future.

  Next year, Cara will go to Rome.

Practice Write the sentences. Write the verb in the future tense.

1. Cara and her family fly in a big plane.

2. The family tours the city.

3. Cara takes many pictures.

4. Cara sees old ruins.

5. Everyone buys presents for friends back home.

RULE 6

Subject-Verb Agreement

- A **present-tense** verb must agree with its subject.

  Two children gather pink flowers.

- Do not add *-s* or *-es* to a present-tense verb when the subject is plural or *I* or *you*.

Practice Write the sentences. Use the correct form of the present-tense verb in ( ).

1. Terry and I (place) flowers on the table.

2. Grandma (thread) two large needles with string.

3. Terry (poke) the needle through each flower.

4. Both of us (work) carefully.

5. We proudly (wear) our flower necklaces.

 QUICK WRITE Write three sentences. Use a present-tense verb in the first, a past-tense verb in the second, and a future-tense verb in the third.

147

Grammar

RULE 7

Main and Helping Verbs

- Sometimes a verb can be more than one word. The main verb tells what the subject does or is.

  Jess is visiting his uncle's ranch.

- The helping verb helps the main verb show an action.

  Jess is visiting his uncle's ranch.

- Use the helping verbs *has, have,* and *had* to help main verbs show an action in the past. In sentences with helping verbs, both the main verb and the helping verb must agree with the subject.

- Use *has* with a singular subject and *he, she,* or *it.*

- Use *have* with a plural subject and *I, you, we,* or *they.*

- Use *had* with a singular or plural subject.

Practice Write the sentences. Draw one line under each main verb. Draw two lines under each helping verb.

1. Jess had flown to Texas in a jet.
2. Uncle Bob is raising cattle.
3. Jess has helped his uncle every summer.
4. This summer Jess is helping Uncle Bob again.
5. Uncle Bob and Aunt Rita have met Jess at the airport.

RULE 8

Contractions with *Not*

- A contraction is a shortened form of two words.

- An apostrophe (') shows where one or more letters have been left out.

Practice Write the new sentences. Write the words that make up each contraction.

1. I can't find my book.

2. It isn't in the bookcase.

3. I don't know where to look.

4. Didn't you see the book?

5. I haven't looked in my room.

RULE 9 **Combining Sentences: Verbs**

• You can join two sentences with the same subject by combining the predicates. Use *and* to join the predicates of two sentences that have the same subject.

Laura loved science. Laura studied the stars.
Laura loved science and *studied the stars.*

Practice Write each pair of sentences as one sentence. Use the word *and* to join the predicates.

1. Nina loved space. Nina wanted to be an astronaut.

2. The space program needed astronauts. The space program accepted Nina.

3. The shuttle lifted off. The shuttle flew to the space station.

4. Nina lived in the space station. Nina stayed six months.

5. The scientists did experiments. The scientists carried out projects.

Grammar

RULE 10 — Irregular Verbs

- An **irregular verb** has a special spelling to show the past tense. Some irregular verbs have a special spelling when used with the helping verb *have*.

Present	Past	Past with *have*, *has*, or *had*
begin	began	begun
bring	brought	brought
come	came	come
eat	ate	eaten
do	did	done
give	gave	given
go	went	gone
grow	grew	grown
run	ran	run
say	said	said
see	saw	seen
sing	sang	sung

Practice Write the sentences. Change each present-tense verb in ( ) to the past tense.

1. Lil and Beth (go) to the movies.

2. The girls (run) all the way.

3. Beth (do) not want to be late.

4. Lil (see) her friend Maria at the movie.

5. Maria had (bring) her brother with her.

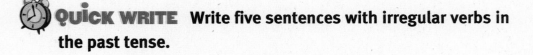 **QUICK WRITE** Write five sentences with irregular verbs in the past tense.

RULE 1 — **Pronouns**

- A **pronoun** is a word that takes the place of one or more nouns.

  Nora plays soccer. She plays soccer.

Practice Rewrite each sentence. Replace the underlined word or words with the correct pronoun in ( ).

1. The children run after the ball. (They, He)

2. Nora kicks the ball toward the goal. (she, it)

3. Lennie cheers when Nora scores. (I, He)

4. Nora waves at Meg and me. (us, them)

5. Will our team win the game? (you, we)

RULE 2 — **Subject Pronouns and Object Pronouns**

- A **subject pronoun** is used as the subject of a sentence.

  Singular subject pronouns: *I, you, he, she, it*
  Plural subject pronouns: *we, you, they*

- Use an **object pronoun** after an action verb or words such as *for, at, of, with,* and *to.*

  Singular object pronouns: *me, you, him, her, it*
  Plural object pronouns: *us, you, them*

Practice Write the sentences. Replace the underlined word or words with a subject pronoun or an object pronoun.

1. Carl told Mark and me about his hobby.

2. Coin collecting interests Carl.

3. Carl showed his coins to Jill.

4. Jill and Carl have pictures of coins.

5. Jill gave a coin book to Mark.

Grammar

RULE 3 — Pronoun-Verb Agreement

- A present-tense action verb must agree with its subject pronoun.

- Add *-s* to most action verbs in the present tense when you use the pronouns *he, she,* and *it.*

- Do not add *-s* to an action verb in the present tense when you use the pronouns *I, we, you,* and *they.*

  He picks blueberries. I pick blueberries.

Practice **Write the sentences. Complete each sentence with the correct verb in ( ).**

1. We (bring, brings) some blueberries home.
2. They (taste, tastes) sweet.
3. You (make, makes) blueberry jam.
4. It (smell, smells) wonderful!
5. I (eat, eats) some bread and jam.

RULE 4 — Possessive Pronouns

- A **possessive pronoun** takes the place of a possessive noun. It shows who or what owns something.

  Walt's game is fun. His game is fun.

- These possessive pronouns are used before nouns:
  my, your, his, her, its, our, their.

  That is their computer.

- These possessive pronouns can stand alone:
  mine, yours, his, hers, its, ours, theirs.

  Is that yours?

Practice Write the sentences. Draw a line under each possessive pronoun.

1. The computer is his.

2. My computer screen changes color.

3. Her fingers are on the keyboard.

4. You can play your computer game.

5. When did you get that game of yours?

RULE 5 ── **Pronoun-Verb Contractions** ──

- A contraction is a shortened form of two words. There are many pronoun–verb contractions.

- An *apostrophe* (') replaces missing letters.

he's = he + is; he + has
she's = she + is; she + has
it's = it + is; it + has
I'm = I + am
you're = you + are
we're = we + are
they're = they + are
I've = I + have
you've = you + have

we've = we + have
they've = they + have
I'll = I + will
he'll = he + will
she'll = she + will
we'll = we + will
you'll = you + will
it'll = it + will
they'll = they + will

Practice Write each sentence. Replace the underlined words with a contraction.

1. She is my sister.

2. He is a friend of mine.

3. They are my cousins.

4. We are part of a large family.

5. It is a family with many children.

⏰ **QUICK WRITE** Write five sentences using nouns in the subject and predicate. Exchange papers. Rewrite the sentences with subject and object pronouns in place of nouns.

Adjectives

Grammar

RULE 1

Adjectives That Tell What Kind or How Many

- An **adjective** is a word that describes a noun.

- Some adjectives tell *what kind* of person, place, or thing the noun is.

  The moon shines in the dark sky.

- Some adjectives tell *how many*.

  Three men enter the spaceship.

- *Few, many,* and *several* are special adjectives that tell *how many*.

  Many people watch the launch on TV.

Practice Write the sentences. Draw one line under each adjective that tells *how many* or *what kind*.

1. One man counts down to blastoff.
2. The long trip begins.
3. Two astronauts step onto the moon.
4. Astronauts study the rocky surface of the moon.
5. Few people have made this trip!

RULE 2

Articles

- **Articles** are special adjectives. The words *a, an,* and *the* are articles.

- Use *a* before singular nouns that begin with a consonant.

- Use *an* before singular nouns that begin with a vowel.

- Use *the* before singular nouns and plural nouns.

Practice Write the sentences. Complete each sentence with the correct article in ( ).

1. Rusty and I play in (the, an) park.

2. I throw (a, an) ball, and Rusty chases it.

3. Rusty brings (a, an) apple back to me.

4. I tell Rusty to get (an, the) ball.

5. Rusty is (a, an) very silly dog!

RULE 3

Adjectives That Compare

- You can use adjectives to compare nouns.

- Add *-er* to an adjective to compare two nouns.

- Add *-est* to compare more than two nouns.

- Some adjectives change their spelling when *-er* or *-est* is added.

- When the adjective ends in a consonant sound and y, change the *y* to *i* and add *-er* or *-est*.

- When the adjective ends in e, drop the *e* and add *-er* or *-est*.

- For adjectives that have a single vowel before a final consonant, double the final consonant and add *-er* or *-est*.

Practice Write the sentences. Add *-er* or *-est* to the adjective in ( ).

1. Dolphins are (small) than killer whales.

2. A crocodile is (big) than an alligator.

3. A sea turtle is (heavy) than a snapping turtle.

4. Whale sharks are the (large) of all fish.

5. Some whales eat the (small) of all fish.

QUICK WRITE Write five sentences with adjectives that compare.

Grammar

Grammar

Adverbs

RULE 1 — Adverbs

- An adverb is a word that tells more about a verb. Adverbs tell *how, when,* or *where* an action takes place.

  Yesterday, dark clouds swiftly moved overhead.

Practice Write *how, when,* or *where* to show what each underlined adverb tells about the verb.

1. Thunder rumbled <u>loudly</u>.

2. Lightning flashed <u>brightly</u>.

3. <u>Next</u>, rain poured from the clouds.

4. I ran <u>inside</u>.

5. <u>Then</u> I dried myself off.

RULE 2 — Adverbs That Tell How

- Some adverbs tell *how* an action takes place.

- Adverbs that tell *how* often end with *-ly*.

  The dog barked loudly.

Practice Write the sentences. Draw a line under each adverb that tells *how*. Draw two lines under the verb it describes.

1. A stray dog walked slowly into town.

2. Mr. Stacy petted the dog gently.

3. The dog wagged his tail excitedly.

4. Mr. Stacy kindly adopted the dog.

5. The dog quickly answered to his new name.

RULE 3

Adverbs That Tell When or Where

- Some adverbs tell *when* or *where* an action takes place.

Practice Write the sentences. Draw a line under each verb. Circle each adverb. Write if the adverb tells *when* or *where*.

1. Vera lost her bike today.

2. She put the bike inside.

3. Vera looked for the bike outdoors.

4. Later, Vera called Wally.

5. Soon, Wally arrived at Vera's house.

RULE 4

Combining Sentences: Adjectives and Adverbs

- Two sentences that tell about the same person, place, or thing can be combined by adding an adjective to one sentence.

   Sylvie heard a noise. It was a loud noise.
   Sylvie heard a loud noise.

- Two sentences that tell about the same action can be combined by adding an adverb to one sentence.

   The trash can fell. It fell noisily.
   The trash can fell noisily.

Practice Add an adjective or adverb to one of the sentences in each pair. Write the new sentence.

1. Sylvie opened the door. She opened it quickly.

2. A raccoon was in the can. The raccoon was fat.

3. The raccoon ran. It ran swiftly.

QUICK WRITE Write five sentences using adverbs that tell *how, when,* or *where.*

Grammar

Abbreviations

Abbreviations are used in informal writing. An **abbreviation** is the shortened form of a word and usually begins with a capital letter and ends with a period.

Titles

- You can abbreviate titles before a name.

Ms. Rose   *Mrs.* Gordon   *Mr.* Martinez   *Dr.* Wong

Practice Write each abbreviation correctly.

1. ms Inez Vasquez
2. dr Ellen Right
3. mrs Karen Inagaki
4. mr Thomas Hale
5. dr Ed Jones

Days of the Week

- You may abbreviate the days of the week.

Sun. Mon. Tues. Wed. Thurs. Fri. Sat.

Months of the Year

- You may abbreviate most months of the year.

Jan. Feb. Mar. Apr. Aug. Sept. Oct. Nov. Dec.

- Do not abbreviate the months *May, June, July.*

Practice Write each abbreviation correctly.

6. tues
7. august
8. Sat
9. jan
10. november
11. Fri
12. apr
13. thursday
14. Wed
15. feb.

States

- In informal writing and on envelopes you may use United States Postal Service Abbreviations for the names of states. There is no period after these abbreviations.

Alabama	AL	Kentucky	KY	North Carolina	NC
Alaska	AK	Louisiana	LA	North Dakota	ND
Arizona	AZ	Maine	ME	Ohio	OH
Arkansas	AR	Maryland	MD	Oklahoma	OK
California	CA	Massachusetts	MA	Oregon	OR
Colorado	CO	Michigan	MI	Pennsylvania	PA
Connecticut	CT	Minnesota	MN	Rhode Island	RI
Delaware	DE	Mississippi	MS	South Carolina	SC
District of Columbia	DC	Missouri	MO	South Dakota	SD
		Montana	MT	Tennessee	TN
Florida	FL	Nebraska	NE	Texas	TX
Georgia	GA	Nevada	NV	Utah	UT
Hawaii	HI	New Hampshire	NH	Vermont	VT
Idaho	ID			Virginia	VA
Illinois	IL	New Jersey	NJ	Washington	WA
Indiana	IN	New Mexico	NM	West Virginia	WV
Iowa	IA	New York	NY	Wisconsin	WI
Kansas	KS			Wyoming	WY

Practice Write the U.S. Postal Service abbreviation for each of the following states.

1. Hawaii

2. Utah

3. Alabama

4. Michigan

5. Vermont

6. Iowa

7. Oregon

8. Louisiana

9. North Dakota

10. Texas

Grammar

Capitalization

---First Word in a Sentence----------------------

- Capitalize the first word in a sentence.

    Spiders have eight legs.

- Capitalize the first word of a direct quotation.
  A quotation is the exact words of a person speaking.

    José said, "Insects have six legs."

---Letters----------------------

- Capitalize all words in a letter's greeting.

    Dear Robin,   *Dear Mr. Henderson:*

- Capitalize the first word in the closing of a letter.

    Yours truly,   *Your friend,*   *Sincerely,*

Practice **Write each item. Use capital letters correctly.**

1. dear aunt juana,

2. "do you like spiders?" asked Louis.

3. some people are afraid of spiders.

4. Tina said, "spiders catch harmful insects."

5. very truly yours,

---Proper Nouns: Names and Titles of People----------------------

- Capitalize names and initials that stand for names.

    Joan Cohen   *T. R. Sullivan*

- Capitalize titles or abbreviations of titles when they come before the names of people.

    Aunt Ada   Mr. Westly   Mayor Gomez

- Capitalize the pronoun *I.*

    My parents and I had a great vacation.

Grammar

Practice **Write the sentences. Use capital letters correctly.**

1. Our family visited uncle chet on his ranch.

2. Mom and i rode horses for the first time.

3. I helped aunt ida clean the stalls.

4. The vet, dr. brand, treated a sick horse.

5. My uncle's neighbor is named k. c. whitby.

Proper Nouns: Names of Places

- Capitalize the names of cities, states, countries, and continents.

    Boston   *Florida*   *China*   *Africa*

- Capitalize the names of geographical features.

    Pacific Ocean   *Loon Mountain*   *Mojave Desert*

- Capitalize the names of streets and highways.

    Grand Avenue   *Route 66*

- Capitalize the names of buildings and bridges.

    Museum of Modern Art   Sears Tower   Brooklyn Bridge

- Capitalize the names of stars and planets.

    Rigel   *Altair*   *Saturn*   *Mars*

Practice **Write the sentences. Use capital letters correctly.**

6. Mark drove to florida last week.

7. Mark enjoyed visiting miami beach.

8. The atlantic ocean was bright blue.

9. Mark took route 1 to the end.

10. The trip over seven mile bridge was exciting.

Grammar

┌─ **Other Proper Nouns** ─────────────────────────┐

- Capitalize the names of schools, clubs, and businesses.

  Frontier School   *4H Club*
  Apex Computers   *Rice Oil Company*

- Capitalize the days of the week, months of the year, and holidays. Do not capitalize the names of the seasons.

  Friday   *July*   *Presidents' Day*   *spring*

- Capitalize abbreviations.

  Dr.   *Mrs.*   *Ave.*   *Rte.*   *Mt.*

- Capitalize the first, the last, and all important words in the title of a book, poem, song, short story, film, and newspaper.

  Robots on the Loose!   *"April Rain"*
  "The Alphabet Song"   *"Harry's Cat"*
  Star Wars   *Washington Post*

└──┘

Practice Write the sentences. Use capital letters correctly.

1. My class at deerfield school is reading a book called *all the presidents*.

2. Our teacher, ms. Choi, showed the film *famous presidents*.

3. Next monday is presidents' day.

4. This holiday comes in february.

5. Today's *deerfield recorder* has a story about president kennedy.

Punctuation

End Marks for Sentences

- A period (.) ends a statement or command.

  There are seals on the ice.
  Hand the field glasses to me.

- A question mark (?) ends a question.

  Do you see any walruses?

- An exclamation mark (!) ends an exclamation.

  Wow, that is a huge walrus!

Periods for Abbreviations

- Use a period to show the end of an abbreviation.

  Mrs.   *Rd.*   *Aug.*

- Use a period with initials.

  P. T. Barnum   L. C. Cox

Practice Write the sentences. Add end marks and periods where they are needed.

1. Mr Shapiro took out his camera
2. Can you get a picture of the baby seals
3. Please don't alarm the seals
4. What a wonderful sight this is
5. How many seals do you see

Grammar

Grammar

Commas in Letters

- Use a **comma** between the names of cities and states.

  Dallas, Texas   *Chicago, Illinois*

- Use a **comma** between the day and the year in dates.

  July 4, 2001   *October 17, 1836*

- Use a **comma** after the greeting and closing in a friendly letter.

  Dear Grandma,   *Yours truly,*

Practice **Add commas where they are needed.**

1. Trenton New Jersey
2. January 1 2002
3. Your friend
4. Dear Uncle Al
5. Kent Ohio

Commas in Sentences

- Use a **comma** to separate words in a series.

  The media center has videos, tapes, and CDs.

- Use a **comma** after the words *yes* and *no* when they begin a sentence.

  Yes, I have read that book.

- Use a comma after the name of a person being spoken to.

  Jill, are you going to the library?

Practice **Add commas where they are needed.**

6. Donna Hal and Kathy are at the library.

7. Hal do you want books on animals?

8. No I want books on baseball soccer and hockey.

9. Donna did you find what you wanted?

10. Yes I found poems stories and novels.

Grammar

Apostrophes

- Use an **apostrophe** (') with nouns to show possession.

- Add an **apostrophe** and an *s ('s)* to singular or plural nouns that do not end in *s*.

  boy's bat   *Tina's ball*   *men's caps*

- Add an **apostrophe** (') to plural nouns ending in *s*.

  games' scores   *players' uniforms*

- Use an **apostrophe** (') in contractions to show where a letter or letters are missing.

  doesn't   *we're*   *you've*   *I'm*

Practice Write the possessive form of the noun in ( ). Write the contraction of the two words in ( ).

1. Baseball (is not) (Jake) favorite game.

2. (I have) gone to all of my (friends) games.

3. Some (children) parents (are not) at the game.

Quotation Marks

- Use **quotation marks** at the beginning and at the end of the exact words a person says.

  "Have you seen my hamster?" asked Sarah.

Practice Add quotation marks where they are needed.

4. The hamster can't have gone far, said Ned.

5. Sarah said, I've looked everywhere.

6. There's my hamster! Sarah cried.

Italics or Underlining

Underline or use *italics* for the title of a book, movie, magazine, or newspaper.

<u>The Cloud Book</u>   *The Lion King*

Extra Practice

Sentences

A. Write the group of words in each pair that is a sentence.

1. The lighthouse is tall. The tall lighthouse.
2. Mia sees the open door. An open door.
3. No light inside. Mia enters the dark building.
4. Mia climbs the stairs. Up the narrow stairs.
5. A long climb. The stairs are steep.
6. Mia grips the railing. Holds on tightly.
7. At the top. Mia gets to the very top.
8. Mia looks out the window. Across the water.
9. The sailboats. Mia sees colorful sailboats.
10. Mia is excited. Sees wonderful things.

B. Write *sentence* if the group of words is a sentence. Write *not a sentence* if the group of words is not a sentence.

11. Fred drove to the bus station.
12. Parked the car.
13. Asked for directions.
14. Fred followed the directions.
15. Fred found his ticket.
16. The bus station was crowded.
17. Fred wanted a book.
18. Went to a gift shop.
19. Bought a book.
20. Fred will get on the bus soon.

Statements and Questions

A. Write each sentence. Write *statement* next to each sentence that tells something. Write *question* next to each sentence that asks something.

1. What grade are you in?
2. I am in third grade.
3. How many boys are in your class?
4. How many girls are in your class?
5. We have a new teacher.
6. Which subject do you like best?
7. I like science.
8. My favorite subject is math.
9. We study music and art in our school.
10. Is Mr. Wilkes the art teacher?

B. Write each sentence. Write *statement* if it is a statement and *question* if it is a question. Add the correct end mark.

11. The class will visit the new museum
12. The Air and Space Museum is in the city
13. When do the children leave on the trip
14. The bus comes at ten o'clock
15. What things will they see in the museum
16. The museum has airplanes from long ago
17. An old plane sits on the floor
18. Can people climb inside the plane
19. Will the guide talk about space travel
20. The children will see a movie about space

Commands and Exclamations

A. Write each sentence. Write *command* next to each sentence that gives an order. Write *exclamation* next to each sentence that shows strong feeling.

1. Look at the rainbow.

2. What a wonderful surprise you will see!

3. Count the different colors in the rainbow.

4. How beautiful the rainbow looks!

5. Make a wish for something special.

6. Watch the rainbow disappear.

7. What a great time we had!

8. Try to learn more about rainbows.

9. Please find a book on rainbows in the library.

10. How many books on rainbows there are!

B. Write each sentence. Write *command* if it is a command and *exclamation* if it is an exclamation. Add the correct end mark.

11. What a great bike that is

12. How nice that color is

13. Take care of your new bike

14. Don't leave your bike outside

15. Wear your helmet when you ride your bike

16. Ask your mom if you can go for a ride

17. Take a ride with me

18. What a great day this is for riding a bike

19. How fast your bike goes

20. Help me fix my bike, please

Sentence Punctuation

A. Write whether each sentence is a *statement*, *question*, *command*, or *exclamation*. Then write the name of the correct end mark for each sentence.

1. Do you want to play ball?

2. What a great idea that is!

3. I'll get my ball and my glove.

4. Bring your new bat, Ashley.

5. Wear your team shirts.

6. The sun is very bright today.

7. Please wear your caps.

8. Take water with you.

9. When will the game begin?

10. How pretty the park looks today!

B. Write each sentence. Begin and end the sentences correctly.

11. ray visited the Alamo

12. have you been to the Alamo

13. the Alamo is in Texas

14. did Davy Crockett fight at the Alamo

15. the Alamo was once a mission

16. what a place the Alamo is

17. what is the famous saying about the Alamo

18. santa Anna was a Mexican general

19. did Santa Anna fight against the Texans

20. find out more about the Alamo

Extra Practice

Subjects in Sentences

A. Write each sentence. Write *subject* next to the sentences in which the subject is underlined.

1. <u>Goldfish</u> live in ponds.

2. Some people keep goldfish in <u>aquariums</u>.

3. People in China breed <u>goldfish</u>.

4. <u>The fantail</u> is a kind of goldfish.

5. Some goldfish have long <u>tails</u>.

6. <u>People</u> buy goldfish for pets.

7. <u>A pet fish</u> needs care.

8. Fish need fresh <u>water</u> and food.

9. <u>The water</u> should be warm.

10. The fish bowl <u>should</u> be clean.

B. Write the sentences. Draw a line under the subject of each sentence.

11. Mexico City is the capital of Mexico.

12. My grandparents live in Mexico City.

13. Many roads lead to Mexico City.

14. The parks are beautiful.

15. Alameda Park has many poplar trees.

16. People shop in outdoor markets.

17. Most newspapers are printed in Spanish.

18. Some newspapers are printed in English.

19. Heavy rains can cause floods.

20. The nights are cool.

Predicates in Sentences

A. Write each sentence. Write *predicate* next to the sentences in which the predicate is underlined.

1. The weather changed quickly.
2. Dark clouds formed in the sky.
3. The strong wind broke tree branches.
4. Lightning streaked across the sky.
5. Thunder broke the silence.
6. Heavy rain poured down on the town.
7. People ran for shelter.
8. Cars splashed water and mud.
9. Umbrellas bent in the wind.
10. The storm lasted a long time.

B. Write each sentence. Draw a line under each predicate.

11. The boat bounced across the water.
12. Waves rocked the boat.
13. The captain turned the wheel.
14. The sailors held the wet ropes.
15. Passengers clung to the rails of the boat.
16. Everyone watched the water.
17. A whale swam next to the boat.
18. Dolphins jumped into the air.
19. Passengers screamed with delight.
20. Water splashed everywhere.

Extra Practice

Combining Sentences

A. Write each sentence. If it is a compound sentence, circle the word that joins the two sentences. If it is not a compound sentence, write *not compound*.

1. The sky is blue, and the clouds are gone.

2. The sun is bright, and the air is warm.

3. There is very little rain, and the ground is dry.

4. Animals dig many holes in the sand.

5. A lizard has a long tail.

6. The children get off the bus, and the teachers meet them.

7. A roadrunner races by, and Maria takes its picture.

8. Linda finds a big cactus, and Vic guesses its age.

9. Desert flowers are colorful.

10. You will not be bored in the desert.

B. Combine each pair of sentences. Write the new compound sentence.

11. The ocean is beautiful. Many people like to visit it.

12. Levi walks along the shore. He feels the sand squishing under his toes.

13. The tide rushes in. The waves are rough.

14. The wind blows the sand. It piles up in dunes.

15. The tide is low. The children can walk for miles.

16. We collect seashells. Some people build sandcastles.

17. Seaweed is an ocean plant. Some sea animals eat it.

18. Dolphins live in the ocean. You can see them playing.

19. Crabs dig in the sand. Shrimp swim in the sea.

20. Lee smells the salty air. She listens to the waves.

Correcting Run-on Sentences

A. **Write each run-on sentence as two sentences.**

1. Sara looked at Brutus he was muddy and wet.

2. Sara filled the tub she wanted to wash her pet.

3. Sara added soap she put the dog in the tub.

4. The dog was covered with bubbles he looked silly.

5. Brutus shook off the bubbles he got Sara all wet.

6. Sara laughed she looked like a marshmallow.

7. Sara washed Brutus carefully she took him out of the tub.

8. Brutus shook himself dry he rolled in the grass.

9. Sara told Brutus to stop he was rolling into the mud.

10. Sara filled the tub again Brutus needed another bath.

B. **Correct each run-on sentence. Write the complete ideas in two separate sentences or rewrite the sentence as a compound sentence.**

11. José ate his lunch then he ran outside.

12. José wanted to play ball his friends were at the ballpark.

13. José grabbed his baseball mitt he got on his bike.

14. José rode his bike fast it was getting dark.

15. Storm clouds rolled across the sky José rode faster.

16. José got to the park the rain began to fall.

17. The baseball teams waited soon the rain stopped.

18. José's team was losing by one run the team needed a hit.

19. José got his turn at bat he was nervous.

20. José had two strikes he wanted his team to win.

Extra Practice

Nouns

A. Write each sentence. Write which of the underlined words are nouns.

1. Six <u>friends</u> <u>went</u> to the <u>fair</u>.
2. The <u>fairgrounds</u> <u>were</u> packed with <u>people</u>.
3. <u>People</u> could <u>buy</u> <u>food</u>, <u>hats</u>, and <u>flags</u>.
4. <u>Pat</u> <u>rode</u> the <u>pony</u>.
5. <u>Brian</u> <u>played</u> several <u>games</u>.
6. <u>Chris</u> <u>found</u> the <u>horses</u> in the <u>barn</u>.
7. <u>Jen</u> <u>ran</u> to pet the <u>rabbits</u>.
8. <u>Sue</u> <u>liked</u> the <u>sheep</u>.
9. <u>Parents</u> and <u>children</u> <u>watched</u> the <u>geese</u>.
10. <u>Families</u> <u>had</u> <u>fun</u> at the <u>fair</u>.

B. Write the sentences. Draw a circle around each noun.

11. The train rolled down the track.
12. The conductor blew the whistle.
13. The train stopped at the station.
14. Passengers stepped onto the platform.
15. Grandparents waved to grandchildren.
16. Other people bought tickets.
17. Travelers carried luggage.
18. The train had six cars and an engine.
19. Each car had many seats.
20. The conductor shut the doors.

Singular and Plural Nouns

A. Write each noun. Write *singular* or *plural* next to each noun.

1. books
2. box
3. dishes
4. glasses
5. truck
6. chairs
7. bike
8. skates
9. lunch
10. sandwiches

B. Write the sentences. Write the plural of each underlined noun.

11. Our family went to some sandy <u>beach</u>.
12. Seth packed three large <u>lunch</u>.
13. I put two <u>towel</u> in the bag.
14. Bill forgot the <u>key</u> to the car.
15. Dad put sunscreen on our <u>shoulder</u>.
16. The lifeguard watched the <u>swimmer</u>.
17. The <u>wave</u> were gentle.
18. Beth built <u>castle</u> in the sand.
19. Jenny flew her <u>kite</u>.
20. I read my <u>book</u>.

Extra Practice

Plural Nouns with -*ies*

A. **Write the sentences. Underline the plural noun in each sentence.**

1. Most cities have more than one library.

2. The ladies walk to the new library.

3. It has two copies of a favorite book.

4. The mysteries are on the top shelf.

5. Many libraries have a computer.

6. I search for short stories.

7. Anna returns a book about bunnies.

8. Joe reads about puppies.

9. Leah finds two old diaries.

10. Families can share a book.

B. **Write the sentences. Write the plural form of each noun in ( ).**

11. The (sky) were clear.

12. There were (butterfly) floating in the air.

13. A ladybug landed on the (daisy).

14. Joe wanted to pick (berry).

15. He took his (puppy) with him.

16. They chased the (bunny).

17. The (blueberry) grew on bushes.

18. Where do (cranberry) grow?

19. The trees were full of (cherry).

20. We shared the fruit with several (family).

More Plural Nouns

A. **Write the sentences. Underline the plural noun in each sentence.**

1. The pond was full of geese.
2. The children ran in the grass.
3. There were several sheep grazing near the pond.
4. Two men were fishing.
5. Dina put her feet in the water.
6. The cold water made her teeth chatter.
7. Women were jogging around the pond.
8. Three moose were sleeping near the pond.
9. I saw some mice in the tall grass.
10. Dan saw two deer near the pond.

B. **Write the sentences. Write the plural form of each underlined noun.**

11. The child went to the zoo.
12. They saw deer with large antlers.
13. Some of them saw sheep in the barn.
14. They saw some mouse inside a wagon.
15. The man helped pull the wagon.
16. The woman rode in the wagon.
17. Wild goose flew over us.
18. The birds have webbed foot.
19. A horse showed its big tooth.
20. We saw moose and elephants.

Extra Practice

Common and Proper Nouns

A. **Write each noun. Write *common* or *proper* next to each one.**

1. Longfellow Elementary School
2. school
3. September
4. blackboard
5. computer
6. Mr. Matthews
7. teacher
8. Friday
9. recess
10. Labor Day

B. **Write each sentence. Draw one line under each common noun. Draw two lines under each proper noun.**

11. Pam and Sam Franks are twins.
12. Samantha is shorter than her sister.
13. Their cousins own Plainview Ranch.
14. Mr. Franks, their father, owns a farm.
15. Mrs. Franks is a teacher at their school.
16. The girls raise pigs.
17. Sam won a prize at the Miller County Fair.
18. The name of her pig is Petunia.
19. Petunia won a blue ribbon in the contest.
20. The family enjoyed the fair on Saturday.

Capitalization

A. Write each proper noun correctly.

1. tuesday
2. memorial day
3. rio grande
4. chicago
5. july

6. abraham lincoln
7. walt disney
8. december
9. thursday
10. san diego zoo

B. Write each sentence. Write the proper nouns correctly.

11. Today is flag day.

12. We read a book called *our first flag*.

13. On wednesday, we will read another book.

14. Ms. davis wrote the book.

15. It is called *state flags*.

16. Did you know betsy ross made the first flag?

17. The flag of the united states has stars and stripes.

18. We celebrate this holiday in june.

19. I read the book *salute to flags* to our class.

20. We will have no school on friday.

Extra Practice

Singular Possessive Nouns

A. Write each singular noun. Write the possessive form of each noun next to it.

1. beaver
2. cat
3. cow
4. bird
5. rabbit
6. dog
7. whale
8. butterfly
9. spider
10. porcupine

B. Write each sentence. Use the possessive form of the noun in ( ).

11. (Rosa) family has a pet dog.
12. The (dog) name is Trouble.
13. (Trouble) name fits him.
14. The dog chewed (Mom) slipper.
15. He stole (Dad) favorite shirt.
16. The (trainer) name is Max.
17. (Max) name is short for Maxine.
18. Trouble is (Maxine) favorite dog.
19. Trouble likes to chase the (family) cat, Lipton.
20. The (cat) favorite hiding place is under my bed.

Plural Possessive Nouns

A. Write the words. Write whether each word is a singular possessive noun or a plural possessive noun.

1. students'
2. boys'
3. lion's
4. bear's
5. bees'

6. groundhog's
7. children's
8. skunks'
9. snakes'
10. Roy's

B. Write each sentence. Use the correct possessive form of the plural noun in ( ).

11. The (players) uniforms are blue.

12. The (referees) shirts are black and white.

13. Two (months) practice has made the players good.

14. Mike read the (coaches) notes.

15. We saw the (managers) names on the notes.

16. Rajah learned about the (catchers) jobs on the field.

17. He visited the (owners) offices.

18. The (trainers) suggestions were good.

19. The (fans) cheers were loud.

20. The (women) team won by one run.

Combining Sentences: Nouns

A. **Write each pair of sentences. Circle the two nouns that you can join with *and* to combine the sentences. Underline the words that repeat.**

1. Whales are mammals. Humans are mammals.
2. Do whales have spouts? Do dolphins have spouts?
3. Abdul likes whales. Abdul likes sharks.
4. Sean likes sharks. Sean likes porpoises.
5. Whales live in the ocean. Porpoises live in the ocean.
6. Are whales dying out? Are porpoises dying out?
7. Abdul lived in the city. Sean lived in the city.
8. Sean likes science. Sean likes reading.
9. Sean reads about fish. Sean reads about mammals.
10. The boys are swimmers. The boys are divers.

B. **Combine each pair of sentences. Use the word *and* to join two nouns. Write the new sentence.**

11. Mia likes animals. Mia likes sports.
12. She has lived in Florida. She has lived in California.
13. Carlos liked the ocean. Mia liked the ocean.
14. Sara watched the seals. Sara watched the seahorses.
15. The seals were playful. The dolphins were playful.
16. Children waved to ships. Parents waved to ships.
17. The girls collected shells. The boys collected shells.
18. The sisters caught crabs. The sisters caught fish.
19. Jamal sailed today. Jim sailed today.
20. Carlos went swimming. Mia went swimming.

Abbreviations

A. Write the abbreviations. Then write what each abbreviation stands for.

1. Sun.

2. Sept.

3. Mr.

4. Thurs.

5. Nov.

6. Sat.

7. Dr.

8. Wed.

9. Aug.

10. Oct.

B. Write each abbreviation correctly.

11. dr.

12. mon

13. mrs

14. Dec

15. tues.

16. gov

17. Apr

18. jan

19. fri

20. feb

Grammar

Action Verbs

A. **Write each sentence. Underline the action verb.**

1. Lucia writes a play.
2. Terrell designs the scenery.
3. His friends make props.
4. Ms. Garza sews the costumes.
5. Kaitlyn creates a program.
6. The crowd enters the hall.
7. The actors wait behind the curtain.
8. The people look toward the stage.
9. Mr. Jones plays the piano.
10. The curtain opens at the sound of music.

B. **Write each sentence. Use the correct word in ( ).**

11. I (joined, noisy) a dance club.
12. My friends (attend, music) dance class every week.
13. The dancers (dress, new) in black tights.
14. We (wear, small) taps on our shoes.
15. Dancers (listen, ears) carefully to the music.
16. I (imagine, idea) a special day.
17. We (dance, song) before a big audience.
18. Everyone (cheers, happy) our performance.
19. I (bow, grateful) in front of the happy crowd.
20. I (awake, surprise) from my dream!

Present-Tense Verbs

A. Write each sentence. Choose the correct verb in ( ).

1. Armando (play, plays) his flute every day.

2. His friend Vera (like, likes) his music.

3. The teacher (listens, listen) to Armando's music.

4. She (write, writes) a letter to a famous flute player.

5. The musician (reply, replies) to the letter.

6. Mr. Shen (visits, visit) the school.

7. The student (meets, meet) the flute player.

8. He (explain, explains) the parts of the flute to Armando.

9. He (teaches, teach) Armando a new piece of music.

10. The principal (invite, invites) Mr. Shen to perform for the school.

B. Write each sentence. Use the correct present-tense form of the verb in ( ). Spell the verb correctly.

11. The musician (carry) his flute to the gym.

12. Vera (rush) to get a front seat.

13. Mr. Shen (hold) the instrument gently.

14. He (press) the keys to play the music.

15. The song (sound) lovely.

16. The teacher (enjoy) the concert.

17. Bruce (hope) to be a singer.

18. He (take) singing lessons every week.

19. The teacher (say) Bruce sings well.

20. Bruce (practice) singing with Armando.

Extra Practice

Subject-Verb Agreement

A. Write the verb in each sentence. If the sentence has a singular subject, write *singular* next to the verb. If the sentence has a plural subject, write *plural*.

1. I notice many birds in our backyard.

2. The birds need food.

3. I build a bird feeder.

4. Ramon and Keisha help me.

5. My friends use pine cones.

6. My neighbors gather many cones.

7. Ramon brings peanut butter.

8. Keisha gets plastic spoons.

9. We spread peanut butter on the pine cones.

10. My brother hangs the pine cones on a tree.

B. Write each sentence. Write the correct present-tense form of the verb in ( ).

11. The birds (love, loves) our peanut butter cones.

12. Ramon, Keisha, and I (make, makes) another bird feeder.

13. I (string, strings) cranberries on a long thread.

14. You (tie, ties) the string of cranberries to another tree.

15. A rabbit (notice, notices) the red cranberries.

16. The animal (reach, reaches) up.

17. The rabbit (chew, chews) the berries on the string.

18. Ramon (climb, climbs) up the tree.

19. He (wrap, wraps) the string of cranberries around a branch.

20. The birds (peck, pecks) at the berries on the tree branch.

Letter Punctuation

A. **Choose the correct item in each pair. Write the letter for your answer.**

1. a. dear Mr. Murphy,   b. Dear Mr. Murphy,

2. a. Dear, Cameron   b. Dear Cameron,

3. a. sincerely Yours, Dan   b. Sincerely yours, Dan

4. a. Your friend, Teri   b. Your, friend Teri

5. a. Dear Skyler,   b. dear Skyler,

6. a. Love Renee,   b. Love, Renee

7. a. Dear, Grandma Kim,   b. Dear Grandma Kim,

8. a. Love, Uncle Ralph   b. love, Uncle Ralph

9. a. yours truly, Tomas   b. Yours truly, Tomas

10. a. Sincerely, Julie   b. Sincerely, Julie,

B. **Write each item correctly.**

11. dear Mrs. Colby

12. Your Cousin Marion

13. most, sincerely Adam

14. Love Aunt JoAnn

15. dear Edmund

16. yours Truly Hayley

17. Dear, Tad

18. very Truly, yours Brooke

19. dear, Mr. Willey

20. love Uncle Stuart

Extra Practice

Past-Tense Verbs

A. Write each sentence. Underline the past-tense verb.

1. It looked like a snowy day.

2. Dad cooked eggs for breakfast.

3. Kenji liked the whole wheat toast.

4. I sipped fresh apple juice.

5. We carried our dishes to the sink.

6. Snowflakes drifted slowly to the ground.

7. Kenji grabbed his snow pants and mittens.

8. I gathered my gloves and scarf.

9. Mom opened the front door.

10. Cold air roared into the warm kitchen.

B. Write each sentence. Use the past tense of the verb in ( ).

11. We (walk) toward the backyard.

12. Kenji (roll) two snowballs.

13. I (stack) the small snowball on top of the big one.

14. The children (dry) their hands.

15. I (fetch) two twigs for the snowman's arms.

16. Kenji (use) a carrot for the snowman's nose.

17. The snowman (smile) with its crooked mouth.

18. The snowman still (need) a scarf.

19. I (plop) a hat on the snowman's head.

20. We (wave) good-bye to our friend.

Future-Tense Verbs

A. **Write each sentence. Write whether each underlined verb is in the *past*, *present*, or *future* tense.**

1. Years ago, people <u>traveled</u> by horse and buggy.

2. They <u>admired</u> the countryside.

3. Horses still <u>pull</u> buggies.

4. Today, people <u>drive</u> cars instead of buggies.

5. A creative person <u>designed</u> a horseless buggy.

6. People <u>enjoyed</u> a new way of traveling.

7. In the future, we <u>will travel</u> in new ways.

8. Someone <u>will invent</u> a faster way to travel.

9. Someday, maybe people <u>will live</u> in outer space.

10. I <u>want</u> a spaceship of my own.

B. **Write each sentence. Write the verb in the future tense.**

11. Our class hosts a science fair.

12. Students display their projects.

13. I enter my spaceship design in the contest.

14. Some projects show designs for the home.

15. Tina invents a new egg cooker.

16. Sheila creates a robot.

17. Mrs. Francis picks the winning entry.

18. The winner receives a ribbon.

19. We celebrate by having a party.

20. The class plans projects for next year's fair.

Combining Sentences: Verbs

A. Write each sentence. Underline the predicate. Circle the word that joins two verbs.

1. Sarah likes and shows pets.

2. She plans and arranges a pet parade.

3. Mel washes and combs his dog.

4. Jody brushes and fluffs her cat's fur.

5. Sarah leads and directs the parade.

6. Some pets show off and do tricks.

7. Valerie's parrot talks and squawks loudly.

8. Jody's cat meows and prances.

9. Mel's dog jumps and spins.

10. The crowd claps and cheers for the funny pets.

B. Combine each pair of sentences. Use *and* to join the two predicates. Write the new sentence.

11. Mom plans a camping trip. Mom arranges a camping trip.

12. Dad buys the food. Dad packs the food.

13. Ana finds the camping gear. Ana sorts the camping gear.

14. Luis chooses some outdoor clothes. Luis packs some outdoor clothes.

15. Mom chops some firewood. Mom stacks some firewood.

16. Mom builds a campfire. Mom lights a campfire.

17. Dad washes some vegetables. Dad cooks some vegetables.

18. Everyone sings after dinner. Everyone plays after dinner.

19. The children toast marshmallows. The children eat marshmallows.

20. The family sleeps under the stars. The family dreams under the stars.

Commas in Dates and Places

A. Choose the correct item in each pair. Write the letter for your answer.

1. a. July 25, 1996   b. July, 25 1996
2. a. Aurora, Illinois   b. Aurora Illinois,
3. a. April 8 1993   b. April 8, 1993
4. a. St., Louis Missouri   b. St. Louis, Missouri
5. a. Nome Alaska   b. Nome, Alaska
6. a. June 18, 1966   b. June 18, 19,66
7. a. January 9, 1954   b. January, 9, 1954
8. a. Seattle, Washington   b. Seattle Washington
9. a. August, 11, 2001   b. August 11, 2001
10. a. Flint Michigan   b. Flint, Michigan

B. Write the sentences. Add commas where they are needed.

11. Lindsey lives in Landview Pennsylvania.
12. She moved there on February 12 1998.
13. Before that, she lived in New York New York.
14. I visited her on August 2 2000.
15. I met her on her birthday in Orlando Florida.
16. I returned home on August 9 2000.
17. Lindsey was born on August 6 1990.
18. My mother was born in Tampa Bay Florida.
19. My favorite city to visit is Toronto Ontario.
20. I went there on December 31 2000.

Main and Helping Verbs

A. Write the underlined verb in each sentence. Write *main verb* or *helping verb* next to it.

1. Our neighborhood <u>is</u> cleaning our park.

2. The parents will <u>bring</u> trash bags.

3. The children <u>will</u> collect the trash.

4. Mike <u>has</u> washed the benches.

5. Nick and Josh are <u>pulling</u> weeds.

6. Lisa and Keiko <u>are</u> sweeping the sidewalk.

7. Some people <u>were</u> building a new sign.

8. My dad has <u>fixed</u> the swing.

9. The girls <u>have</u> planted some flowers.

10. We will <u>keep</u> our park clean.

B. Write each sentence. Draw one line under each main verb. Draw two lines under each helping verb.

11. Our neighborhood is planning a block party.

12. Each family will make a booth.

13. Mr. Diaz has created a bean bag game.

14. Sammy and Juan are arranging the prizes.

15. My family will run a ring toss.

16. I am making the rings with rope.

17. The Santanas have finished a fruit stand.

18. Mrs. Santana was bringing the apples.

19. The boys were painting the sign.

20. Everyone will enjoy the games.

Using Helping Verbs

A. Write each sentence. Use the correct helping verb in ( ).

1. Dad (has, have) cooked a delicious meal.

2. We (had, has) asked Dad to make the meal.

3. I (have, has) helped to prepare the food.

4. You (have, has) eaten more than my brother.

5. My brother (had, have) eaten some grapes earlier.

6. My sisters (have, has) surprised us with a dessert.

7. My sisters (had, has) baked an apple pie.

8. Mom (have, has) tasted the pie.

9. She (had, have) saved room for dessert.

10. My brother and I (had, has) eaten too much.

B. Write each sentence. Use the correct form of the main verb in ( ).

11. The students have (visit, visited) an apple farm.

12. The farmer had (stacks, stacked) boxes of apples.

13. The seeds have (form, formed) a star in the apple.

14. A worker has (picking, picked) some apples.

15. The workers have (poured, pour) the apples into a tub.

16. Some workers have (wash, washed) the apples.

17. They have (shined, shone) some apples.

18. The farmer has (slice, sliced) an apple.

19. We have (taste, tasted) the apples.

20. Many visitors had (walked, walks) through the orchard.

Extra Practice

Linking Verbs

A. Write the underlined verb in each sentence. Write *linking verb* or *action verb* next to it.

1. The Nature Park <u>is</u> colorful in the fall.

2. The leaves <u>change</u> colors.

3. The leaves <u>are</u> orange, yellow, and brown.

4. The fallen leaves <u>crackle</u> under our feet.

5. The moss <u>grows</u> on the trees.

6. Many animals <u>live</u> in the park.

7. I <u>hear</u> the birds in the trees.

8. The mother bird <u>is</u> blue and gray.

9. I <u>watch</u> the squirrels.

10. The squirrels <u>are</u> so playful.

B. Write each sentence. Draw a line under each verb. Write *linking verb* or *action verb* to describe each verb.

11. The Nature Park is beautiful in the winter.

12. The snow covers the trees.

13. Everything is fresh and clean.

14. The air was cold and clear.

15. My hair was white with snowflakes.

16. My sister and I leave footprints in the snow.

17. I make a snow castle.

18. The snow castle is lovely.

19. My sister builds a snowman.

20. The snowman is big and round.

Using Linking Verbs

A. **Write the underlined verb in each sentence. Write whether the subject is *singular* or *plural*.**

1. My cousin <u>is</u> captain of the swim team.
2. He <u>is</u> a good swimmer.
3. Last year, he <u>was</u> the fastest swimmer on his team.
4. His teammates <u>were</u> proud of him.
5. I <u>am</u> proud of him.
6. The team's swimsuits <u>are</u> blue and white.
7. The swimmers <u>are</u> fine athletes.
8. They <u>are</u> ready to race.
9. The race <u>is</u> over quickly.
10. My cousin <u>is</u> the winner again.

B. **Write each sentence. Use the correct verb in ( ).**

11. Last week, my friends and I (was, were) at the lake.
12. The lake (was, were) very cold.
13. We (was, were) swimming in the lake.
14. Soon they (was, were) shivering from cold.
15. The lake (is, are) very calm after their swim.
16. I (am, are) tired after swimming in the lake.
17. My sister and I (is, are) at the pool today.
18. My brother (is, are) a good swimmer.
19. You (am, are) a better swimmer than my sister.
20. All my friends (is, are) good swimmers.

Commas in a Series

A. Write each sentence. Underline the words in a series. Circle the commas.

1. My father, sisters, and I went to a football game.

2. Teri, Olga, and Jamie know a lot about football.

3. I learned about touchdowns, touchbacks, and field goals.

4. Our favorite teams are the Bears, Broncos, and Cowboys.

5. The Broncos' colors are blue, orange, and white.

6. The quarterback caught, aimed, and threw the ball.

7. The team ran, blocked, and tackled the other team.

8. The players could catch, run, and throw well.

9. The cheerleaders, fans, and announcers enjoyed the game.

10. The trucks, vans, and cars left the parking lot.

B. Write each sentence. Add commas where they belong.

11. Ethan Bruno and Janel like basketball.

12. Bruno cheers stomps and claps for his favorite team.

13. Janel's favorite teams are the Bulls Jazz and Hornets.

14. The coaches watch pace and call plays for the teams.

15. Basketball players dribble pass and shoot the ball.

16. The basketball bounces soars and sinks into the net.

17. The fans shout scream and cheer for their team.

18. The team scored one two and three points.

19. The basketball player runs jumps and grabs the ball.

20. Our favorite team scores wins and celebrates.

Irregular Verbs

A. **Write each sentence. Underline the irregular verb.**

1. My family went to a campground.

2. The ranger had seen bears nearby.

3. We saw a big bear.

4. The bear had come for food.

5. The bear came too close.

6. We did nothing.

7. The ranger had gone home.

8. The bear ran into the forest.

9. We went into our tent.

10. I have seen enough bears.

B. **Write each sentence. Change each present-tense verb in ( ) to the past tense.**

11. Our family (see) some animals at the camp.

12. Most of the animals (run) away.

13. A duck (go) into the lake.

14. Two squirrels (come) close to us.

15. A deer (go) by our tent.

16. My mother (say) to stand still.

17. The deer (come) closer to us.

18. My brother (say) something.

19. The deer (run) away quickly.

20. I (see) many animals.

Grammar

More Irregular Verbs

A. **Write each sentence. Underline the irregular verb.**

1. The bicycle parade had begun in the morning.

2. Our family picnic began after the parade.

3. All of my relatives had brought food for the picnic.

4. Grandpa brought some fruit to the picnic.

5. Everyone ate plenty of food.

6. Our dog has eaten the scraps of food.

7. My cousin had grown two inches taller since last year.

8. My cousin has given me his old bike.

9. My dad gave his nieces stickers for their bikes.

10. Aunt Carmela sang the song "Bicycle Built for Two."

B. **Write each sentence. Change each present-tense verb in ( ) to the past tense.**

11. My mom and I (give) our neighbor a "Welcome" party.

12. The party (begin) at noon on Saturday.

13. We (eat) meatballs and pasta soup.

14. Our neighbor (bring) dessert for everyone.

15. My aunt (bring) flowers to the party.

16. Beautiful flowers (grow) in my aunt's garden.

17. My sister and I (give) our new neighbor a poem.

18. We (sing) our favorite songs.

19. Our new neighbor (begin) to feel at home.

20. Later, everyone (go) home.

Contractions With *Not*

A. **Write the sentences. Write the words that make up each underlined contraction.**

1. I <u>haven't</u> heard from my friend.

2. My friend <u>hasn't</u> written for a while.

3. My friend <u>didn't</u> send me a letter.

4. Maybe my letters <u>haven't</u> reached my friend.

5. I wonder if my friend <u>didn't</u> get to the mailbox.

6. Perhaps my friend <u>doesn't</u> have any stamps.

7. Maybe my friend <u>isn't</u> living at the same address.

8. I <u>can't</u> wait to get a letter from my friend.

9. I <u>won't</u> stop writing letters to my friend.

10. I <u>haven't</u> tried to call my friend yet.

B. **Write each sentence. Change the underlined words to a contraction.**

11. Our mail <u>has not</u> arrived yet.

12. I <u>cannot</u> wait for the mail.

13. The mail <u>is not</u> usually late.

14. The mail carrier <u>was not</u> feeling well.

15. I <u>have not</u> seen our mail carrier today.

16. Our mail carrier <u>did not</u> skip work.

17. Our mail carrier <u>has not</u> missed a day.

18. I <u>do not</u> want another mail carrier.

19. A mail carrier's job <u>is not</u> easy.

20. I hope she <u>will not</u> be sick for long.

Grammar

Combining Sentences: Verbs

A. Write each sentence. Draw a line under the two predicates. Circle the word that joins the predicates.

1. Benito visited the museum and learned about space.

2. Benito saw pictures of the moon and touched some moon rocks.

3. The museum guide pointed to the sky and showed us some stars.

4. We looked through a telescope and studied the planets.

5. Benito opened a door and walked through a spaceship.

6. We talked with an astronaut and asked him questions.

7. The astronaut answered questions and told us about space.

8. Astronauts wear spacesuits and eat special foods.

9. Astronauts need special training and study hard.

10. We all enjoyed the museum and learned a lot about space.

B. Combine each pair of sentences. Use *and* to join the two predicates. Write the new sentence.

11. Astronauts travel in rockets. Astronauts explore space.

12. Astronauts landed on the moon. Astronauts placed a flag.

13. The crew trains hard. The crew faces many tests.

14. The crew enters the shuttle. The crew checks the controls.

15. The crew works together. The crew completes the checks.

16. The shuttle takes off. The shuttle uses lots of fuel.

17. The crew mends space stations. The crew fixes satellites.

18. Satellites orbit Earth. Satellites send information.

19. The crew finishes the job. The crew returns to Earth.

20. The crew is tired. The crew is glad to be home.

Apostrophes

A. **Write each sentence. Underline the word that has an apostrophe. Write *P* if the word shows possession or *C* if the word is a contraction.**

1. Mr. Caruso's class is interesting.

2. My sister doesn't understand her homework.

3. We sit at Mother's desk to study.

4. I look over my sister's homework.

5. There weren't many mistakes in the homework.

6. The homework wasn't too hard.

7. My sister won't need much help with her homework.

8. I haven't finished my homework.

9. My brothers' homework is complete.

10. Our teacher checks my friend's homework.

B. **Write each sentence. Change each word or words in ( ) to show possession or to show a contraction.**

11. My friend and I went to my (teachers) story hour.

12. I enjoy listening to the (readers) voice.

13. She read my (friends) favorite book.

14. The story is about many (pirates) treasure.

15. The story (is not) my favorite.

16. My favorite story (does not) have pirates.

17. I like the story about a (girls) adventure at sea.

18. My friend (did not) see the pictures.

19. My book (does not) have many pictures.

20. My friend and I (cannot) waituntil the next story hour.

Extra Practice

Pronouns

A. Write the sentences. Underline each pronoun.

1. Do you hear Fritz meowing?

2. He is up in the tree.

3. Hans and Elsa called to him.

4. They hummed Fritz's favorite tune.

5. We listened to Hans and Elsa.

6. The kitten watched them.

7. Then Fritz looked at me.

8. Is he afraid of us?

9. I waved a tuna treat.

10. It brought Fritz down the tree!

B. Write each sentence. Replace the underlined word or words with the correct pronoun in ( ).

11. Miguel and Rosita pack for a vacation. (He, They)

12. Mother gave one suitcase to each child. (She, We)

13. The suitcases fill up fast! (It, They)

14. Miguel arranges shirts and jeans on one side. (He, We)

15. A softball and glove fit on the other side. (It, They)

16. Rosita puts her skates in with the clothes. (She, You)

17. The child can't close the bag. (him, it)

18. The children unpack Rosita's clothes. (She, They)

19. Rosita puts the skates in a backpack. (it, them)

20. Now the bag will close. (he, it)

Subject Pronouns

A. Write each sentence. Underline the subject pronoun.

1. We made a chart of our favorite fruit.

2. I drew a picture of a banana.

3. She found a photo of a basket of apples.

4. He drew a picture of some peaches and plums.

5. They painted bunches of grapes.

6. How will we arrange the pictures on the chart?

7. She pasted the fruit pictures in a circle.

8. He printed "Favorite Fruit" inside the circle.

9. It looks bright and colorful!

10. You will like our nice chart.

B. Write the sentences. Replace each underlined subject with a subject pronoun.

11. The children are making a birthday calendar.

12. Pablo and Ramon collect the names and dates.

13. Elsa creates the calendar on the computer.

14. Carl puts each name in the computer.

15. Angelo and Maria place each name on the right date.

16. The children want pictures on the calendar, too.

17. Ramon looks for the class photos.

18. The photos are kept in a box.

19. Carl scans each picture into the computer.

20. Elsa places a picture above each name.

Extra Practice

Object Pronouns

A. Write each sentence. Underline the object pronoun.

1. Juan and Brigitte play tennis with us.
2. Gil and I face them across the net.
3. Brigitte throws the tennis ball to us.
4. Gil will hit the ball to them.
5. They will teach us.
6. Gil and I watch them carefully.
7. Gil hits it over the fence!
8. Juan throws it back.
9. Brigitte moves next to him.
10. Gil and I will not beat them.

B. Write each sentence. Replace the underlined word or words with an object pronoun.

11. Juan and Brigitte play soccer with Gil and me.
12. Brigitte kicks the soccer ball down the field.
13. Juan passes the ball to Brigitte.
14. Gil kicks the ball away from Juan and Brigitte.
15. Juan blocks Gil.
16. Gil runs in front of Juan.
17. Gil sees the goal and runs toward the goal.
18. I help Gil keep the ball from Brigitte.
19. I kick the ball right into the goal!
20. Juan and Brigitte thank Gil and me for a great game.

Using *I* and *Me*

A. Write the sentences. Write whether the underlined pronoun is *in the subject* or *in the predicate.*

1. I like my new school.

2. Today is a big day for me.

3. My new friend Eva takes me to the gym.

4. I sign up for the team.

5. Eva and I fill out a form.

6. I bring the form to the coach.

7. The coach smiles at Eva and me.

8. He will teach me the game.

9. The coach throws the ball to me.

10. I shoot the basketball into the basket.

B. Write the sentences. Use the correct pronoun in ( ).

11. Eva and (I, me) live near each other.

12. Eva and (I, me) walk to basketball practice together.

13. My mom takes Eva and (I, me) home after practice.

14. Eva and (I, me) are both forwards on the basketball team.

15. The coach helps Eva and (I, me) during practice.

16. Eva and (I, me) shoot baskets.

17. Many players will be on the team with Eva and (I, me).

18. Eva and (I, me) meet a new girl at basketball practice.

19. The coach and (I, me) help the new player shoot baskets.

20. The new girl will be on the team with Eva and (I, me).

Grammar

Pronoun-Verb Agreement

A. Write each sentence. Use the verb in ( ) that agrees with the underlined subject pronoun.

1. <u>He</u> (borrow, borrows) some tools.
2. <u>She</u> (show, shows) Henri the broken wood.
3. <u>We</u> (give, gives) Henri some new pieces of wood.
4. <u>He</u> (mend, mends) the hole in the fence.
5. <u>You</u> (fix, fixes) the fence.
6. <u>We</u> (pack, packs) up the tools.
7. <u>They</u> (sweep, sweeps) the floor.
8. <u>We</u> (make, makes) him some lemonade.
9. <u>I</u> (thank, thanks) him for his help.
10. <u>He</u> (take, takes) a nap.

B. Write each sentence. Use the correct present-tense form of the verb in ( ).

11. He (find) old toys in the attic.
12. They (throw) out the broken toys.
13. She (keep) most of the toys.
14. We (need) a new home for these toys.
15. I (clean) the toys with soap and water.
16. Can you (fix) the broken toys?
17. We (paint) the toys many bright colors.
18. He (tie) a yellow bow around each toy.
19. They (place) the toys in a big box.
20. It (say) Toys for Kids on the outside of the box.

Possessive Pronouns

A. Write the sentences. Underline the possessive pronoun in each sentence.

1. Which is your favorite place?

2. My favorite place is the state of Texas.

3. Our family lives in Dallas.

4. The brick house on the street is ours.

5. Her house is behind those trees.

6. My best friend lived in a green house.

7. His family lives in Austin now.

8. They love its pretty lakes and green hills.

9. Their family will visit us.

10. He misses his old friends in Dallas.

B. Write each sentence. Use the correct possessive pronoun in ( ).

11. Mom and Dad packed (their, theirs) big suitcase.

12. (Our, Its) driving time was four hours.

13. The new van is faster than (their, theirs).

14. I followed the route on (his, its) map.

15. I left (my, mine) at home.

16. The city appears before (my, mine) eyes.

17. A river winds through (its, his) center.

18. Aunt Rosa's home is (our, ours) for this weekend.

19. (Its, Her) sister has a toy store in town.

20. (Their, Theirs) house is full of toys.

Extra Practice

Pronoun-Verb Contractions

A. Write the sentences. Draw one line under the contraction in each sentence. Write the two words that make up each contraction.

1. We've put the mother and her puppies in a large box.
2. They're only two weeks old.
3. They've opened their eyes at last.
4. She's a good mother.
5. He's playing with the puppies.
6. We're taking turns watching them.
7. I've taken some pictures of the puppies.
8. I'll be happy that I did.
9. They'll grow very fast from now on.
10. You'll have to see the puppies soon!

B. Write each sentence. Replace the underlined words with the correct contraction.

11. They are old enough to leave now.
12. You have asked to keep one of the puppies.
13. He is the puppy with brown spots.
14. You are the first to ask for that puppy.
15. I have saved this puppy for you.
16. We are taking the puppy to the vet today.
17. He will give the puppy its shots.
18. We will have the puppy's fur washed and trimmed.
19. I will put the puppy on a leash for you.
20. I hope you will pick a good name for your pet.

Contractions and Possessive Pronouns

A. **Write each sentence. Write *contraction* or *possessive pronoun* to describe each underlined word.**

1. Their rabbits are cute.

2. They're always hungry.

3. I hope your grocery list includes more rabbit food.

4. You're going to need help with all those bags.

5. A rabbit uses its nose and eyes to find food.

6. It's a big bag of lettuce.

7. They're always asking for more food.

8. What is their favorite food?

9. You're supposed to feed them twice a day.

10. I like your friendly rabbits very much.

B. **Write each sentence. Choose the correct word in ( ) to complete each sentence.**

11. A good class depends on (its, it's) teacher and students.

12. (They're, Their) going to have a new art teacher this year.

13. (Its, It's) fun to teach art.

14. Most students like to share (they're, their) art.

15. (They're, Their) adding two more art classes.

16. (You're, Your) going to love Miss Jewel's art class.

17. Will you show me (you're, your) drawings?

18. (Its, It's) a good way to learn new ideas.

19. Some of (they're, their) drawings make me laugh.

20. (You're, Your) best ideas can come from sharing with others.

Extra Practice

Adjectives That Tell What Kind

A. Write each sentence. Write the adjective that describes each underlined noun.

1. China is a huge <u>country</u>.
2. There are high <u>mountains</u> in parts of China.
3. There are dry <u>deserts</u> in the north.
4. Rice is a favorite <u>food</u> in the south.
5. In the north, wheat is a popular <u>grain</u>.
6. Northern China has cold <u>winters</u>.
7. Southeastern China has warm <u>weather</u>.
8. Bicycles fill the noisy <u>streets</u> of the cities.
9. Trains and boats carry people and useful <u>goods</u>.
10. Visitors go to the famous <u>places</u>.

B. Write each sentence. Draw one line under each adjective. Draw two lines under the noun that the adjective describes.

11. Camels are helpful animals.
12. They carry heavy loads.
13. The animals have strong legs.
14. They are interesting creatures.
15. We enjoy the bumpy ride on a camel.
16. Camels have long eyelashes.
17. The eyelashes protect a camel's big eyes.
18. Hungry camels eat hay and grain.
19. They like to drink cool water.
20. Camels store food and water in their large humps.

Adjectives That Tell How Many

A. **Write the sentences. Write the adjective in each sentence that tells how many.**

1. The farmer has many animals.

2. The pig has seven piglets.

3. Two goats play in the field.

4. A few roosters crow loudly.

5. Several hens have laid eggs.

6. One hen has chicks.

7. The farmer owns many sheep.

8. Several lambs stay by their mothers.

9. The busy farmer milks five cows.

10. A few ducks swim in the big pond.

B. **Write each sentence. Draw one line under each adjective that tells how many. Draw two lines under the noun that the adjective describes.**

11. Many children go into the red barn.

12. There are brown saddles on three horses.

13. Several children ride the gentle horses.

14. The happy children ride for fifteen minutes.

15. The tired horses rest for a few hours.

16. One horse has black spots.

17. Five girls go to the pretty pond.

18. The girls see a few ducks.

19. There are two white ducks on the pond.

20. Rachel feeds one hungry duck.

Extra Practice

Articles

A. Write the sentences. Draw a line under the article or articles in each sentence.

1. An oak tree grew by the pond.
2. The roots of an oak tree go deep into the ground.
3. The branches of the tree spread out wide.
4. Birds build nests in the tree.
5. An owl makes its home in the tree.
6. A swing hangs from one branch of the tree.
7. My father made the swing with a tire.
8. My friends and I enjoy playing on the swing.
9. We collect the acorns that drop from the oak tree.
10. We play in the leaves in the fall.

B. Write the sentences. Complete each sentence with the correct article in ( ).

11. Our family went to (a, the) Animal Park.
12. We saw (a, the) animals in their own habitats.
13. I enjoyed watching (a, an) elephant eat peanuts.
14. My brother enjoyed (the, a) African adventure ride.
15. We ate lunch by (the, a) ape's cage.
16. Mother packed (a, an) sandwich for each of us.
17. After lunch we shared (an, a) orange.
18. We took (a, an) tram across the Animal Park.
19. Dad took a photo of (a, an) alligator.
20. The alligator had (a, an) long tail.

Adjectives That Compare

A. Write the sentences. Use the correct adjective in ( ).

1. The (greater, greatest) zoo of all is the Animal Park.

2. This park is the (newer, newest) zoo in our state.

3. The Animal Park is (smaller, smallest) than the city zoo.

4. The grass is the (greener, greenest) in town.

5. The safari ride is the (longer, longest) ride in the park.

6. The animal cages seem (taller, tallest) than the cages at other zoos.

7. The water in the pond is the (cleaner, cleanest) of all.

8. The elephants are (louder, loudest) than the lions.

9. The bears are (quieter, quietest) than the monkeys.

10. The workers at the park are the (kinder, kindest) people.

B. Write the sentences. Use the correct form of the adjective in ( ).

11. We had the (smart) guide in the Animal Park.

12. The lion keeper is the (strong) worker in the park.

13. The guide gave us the (clear) information.

14. Do you know which animal is the (fast) of all?

15. A cheetah is (fast) than a lion.

16. The snake is one of the (long) animals.

17. The giraffe is the (tall) animal.

18. The spider is one of the (small) animals.

19. A lion is (short) than an elephant.

20. The tortoise has a (long) life than many animals.

Grammar

Spelling Adjectives That Compare

A. Write each sentence. Look at the underlined adjective. Circle the letter that is changed, doubled, or dropped when -er or -est is added. Write the correct spelling of the adjective when the ending in ( ) is added.

1. The weather for this year's field day is <u>sunny</u>. (-er)

2. Last year, the weather was <u>cloudy</u>. (-er)

3. The track was <u>wet</u> last year. (-er)

4. Blue Ridge School has the <u>big</u> playing field. (-est)

5. Our school has the <u>nice</u> pool. (-est)

6. The swim lanes are <u>wide</u>. (-er)

7. The swimmers think the water is <u>icy</u> today. (-er)

8. The other team's basketball players are <u>big</u>. (-er)

9. Most of our football players are <u>heavy</u>. (-er)

10. The <u>speedy</u> runners are the girls. (-est)

11. The <u>tiny</u> skater won a medal. (-est)

12. The <u>thin</u> soccer player kicked a goal. (-est)

13. The bike riders are <u>safe</u> with helmets. (-er)

14. Your school has the <u>noisy</u> fans. (-est)

15. The <u>wise</u> judges give the medals. (-est)

B. **Write the sentences. Add *-er* or *-est* to the adjective in ( ). Use the correct spelling.**

16. Our family went to a carnival on the (busy) day of the summer.

17. My brother Antonio is often the (lucky) one in the family.

18. Antonio found the (speedy) line for the ride.

19. We went on the (big) Ferris wheel I've ever seen.

20. I was (brave) than my brother.

21. My sister Anna was (happy) on the roller coaster.

22. The house of mirrors was the (scary) place.

23. We saw the (funny) circus act.

24. A clown was wearing the (baggy) outfit in the show.

25. The (silly) clown gave each of us a bunch of balloons.

26. Antonio's balloons were (big) than mine.

27. At lunch, I got a (tiny) hamburger than Antonio did.

28. Antonio got the (hot) bag of popcorn.

29. My sister ate the (juicy) apple of all.

30. My brother and sister are the (fine) people I know.

Extra Practice

Using Commas

A. Write each sentence. Underline the word that is followed by a comma.

1. Mom, can I make a sandwich?

2. Yes, you can eat lunch now.

3. Katie, would you help me please?

4. Sure, I will get the bread to make a sandwich.

5. Okay, I will get the peanut butter and jelly.

6. Katie, you can spread the peanut butter on the bread.

7. No, I have never had peanut butter and jelly on toast.

8. Yes, the sandwich is delicious.

9. Orlando, would you like your sandwich on toast?

10. No, I would like my sandwich untoasted.

B. Write each sentence. Add a comma where it is needed.

11. Sydney do you know sign language?

12. Yes my cousin taught me sign language.

13. Okay let me show you the alphabet in sign language.

14. Carlos now let me show you how to sign words.

15. Reggie let's practice signing whole sentences.

16. Marie you are learning sign language quickly.

17. Sydney do you speak any other languages?

18. No I only speak English and American Sign Language.

19. Okay I will teach you to speak Spanish.

20. Carlos I can't wait to learn Spanish.

Adverbs

A. **Write each sentence. Write whether the underlined adverb tells *where*, *when*, or *how*.**

1. The campers sleep <u>peacefully</u>.

2. The stars twinkle <u>brightly</u>.

3. Shooting stars sail <u>quickly</u> across the sky.

4. The moon shines <u>overhead</u>.

5. The forest animals fall asleep <u>quietly</u>.

6. An owl hoots <u>softly</u>.

7. The sun rises <u>early</u>.

8. Birds sing <u>nearby</u>.

9. The campers <u>slowly</u> awaken.

10. <u>Now</u> the stillness of the forest disappears.

B. **Write each sentence. Underline the adverb. Write whether it tells *where*, *when*, or *how*.**

11. Soon the campers will go on a hike.

12. Always take water on a hike.

13. The water bottles are kept here.

14. Fill your bottles completely.

15. Everyone packs for a hike carefully.

16. The trail leads there.

17. The hikers walk slowly.

18. They look down.

19. Hikers need breaks often.

20. The campers return safely.

Grammar

Adverbs That Tell How

A. Write each sentence. Underline the adverb that tells how.

1. The wind blows gently.

2. The clouds move quickly.

3. The storm starts wildly.

4. The rain falls rapidly.

5. The hail bounces noisily against the roof.

6. The thunder crashes loudly.

7. Suddenly, the storm stops.

8. The clouds disappear swiftly.

9. The sun shines brightly.

10. The rainbow stretches beautifully across the sky.

B. Write each sentence. Draw one line under the adverb that tells how. Then draw two lines under the verb it describes.

11. The sun shines directly on the lake.

12. The lake sparkles brightly.

13. The fish jump high.

14. My friend and I sit quietly on the dock.

15. We anxiously wait.

16. My fishing pole moves suddenly.

17. A fish blindly takes the bait.

18. I quickly grab the fishing line.

19. A small fish hangs helplessly on the fishing hook.

20. I carefully free the fish.

Adverbs That Tell When or Where

A. Write each sentence. Write if the underlined adverb tells *where* or *when*.

1. The divers finished the training <u>yesterday</u>.

2. <u>Today</u>, they will make their first dive.

3. All the divers arrived <u>early</u>.

4. <u>First</u>, they checked their air tanks.

5. The divers <u>then</u> boarded the boat.

6. The boat took them <u>out</u> to sea.

7. <u>Soon</u>, they will arrive at the diving spot.

8. Another boat floats <u>nearby</u>.

9. The divers go into the water <u>now</u>.

10. The swimmers look <u>around</u>.

B. Write the sentences. Draw a line under each verb. Draw two lines under each adverb that tells *where* or *when* the action takes place.

11. Alex will dive first.

12. Next, Tara dives.

13. Franklin jumps there.

14. Soon, Alex is breathing easily.

15. He swims down.

16. Tara sees him underwater.

17. Franklin dives last.

18. Finally, the other divers follow.

19. The pleased instructor waits nearby.

20. Later, the happy divers describe their dives.

Extra Practice

Combining Sentences: Adjectives and Adverbs

A. Combine each pair of sentences by adding the underlined adjective or adverb to one sentence. Write the new sentence.

1. The children gather around the piñata. They are <u>excited</u>.

2. The piñata is full of prizes. The piñata is <u>colorful</u>.

3. The children swing the bat. They swing the bat <u>hard</u>.

4. The piñata does not break. The piñata is <u>tough</u>.

5. My brother misses the piñata. My brother is <u>big</u>.

6. My cousin hits the piñata. My cousin hits it <u>harder</u>.

7. The prizes spill on the floor. The floor is <u>messy</u>.

8. The children dive for the prizes. The children dive <u>quickly</u>.

9. Everyone loves the prizes. The prizes are <u>great</u>.

10. The children play with the prizes. They play <u>happily</u>.

B. Combine each pair of sentences by adding an adverb or adjective to one sentence. Write the new sentence.

11. The children play a game. They play it next.

12. My mother plays the music. She plays it loudly.

13. Everyone marches around the chairs. There are ten chairs.

14. The music stops. It stops suddenly.

15. The children rush for a chair. The children are eager.

16. I find a chair. The chair is free.

17. My brother finds a chair. My brother's chair is nearby.

18. The boy waits for the music. He is laughing.

19. The game will end. It will end soon.

20. My brother wins the game. The game is difficult.

Quotation Marks

A. **Write each sentence. Underline the exact words being said.**

1. "Does anyone want to go swimming?" Mother asked.

2. "We will go swimming," my sister and I answered.

3. "Loni, get the towels," Mother said.

4. "I will get the sunscreen," I offered.

5. "I will make some lunch," Mother added.

6. "Can we have turkey sandwiches?" my sister asked.

7. Mother replied, "Yes."

8. "I'm ready now," my sister shouted.

9. "So am I," I said.

10. "Let's go!" we exclaimed.

B. **Write each sentence. Add quotation marks where they are needed.**

11. It is a nice day for swimming, Mother said.

12. Don't go out too far, Mother warned.

13. We won't, my sister and I promised.

14. Do you want to race? my sister asked.

15. No running! the lifeguard yelled.

16. Mother, watch me swim, I called.

17. Mother called back, You are doing great!

18. I cannot hear you, I shouted.

19. You are doing great, my mother repeated.

20. Let's come to the pool again tomorrow, my sister said.

Build Skills

Dictionary

DEFINITIONS

- A dictionary is a book that gives the definitions, or meanings, of words.

- Entry words are the words that are explained in a dictionary. All the words are in alphabetical order.

- Often, a word may have more than one meaning. Each meaning of a word is numbered in a dictionary.

- An example sentence shows one way to use the entry word.

- Guide words at the top of each page show the first and last entry words on the page.

- The part of speech tells how the word can be used in a sentence as a noun, verb, adjective, and so on.

Guide words

Entry word · · · **knowledge** 1. An understanding that comes *Definition* · · · with experience or study: *I have enough knowledge of football to be able to follow the game.* 2. The fact of knowing: *Example sentence* · · · *The knowledge that the car could slide on the icy road made the driver more careful.* **know•ledge** (nol´ij) noun.
Part of speech · · · · · · · · · · · · · · · ·

knowledge / kookaburra

koala A furry, chubby, tree-dwelling animal that lives in Australia. It has grayish-blue fur, large bushy ears, a black nose, and hands that help it grasp the limbs of trees. **ko•a•la** (kō ä´lə) *noun, plural* **koalas**.

Practice Answer the questions about the dictionary.

1. What are the two guide words on the page?

2. Is *koala* a noun or a verb?

3. What are two meanings of the word *knowledge*?

4. What is the last word on this page?

5. Would the word *knot* come before or after this page?

Card Catalog

Build Skills

DEFINITIONS

- The card catalog contains information about all of the books in the library.

- Each book has a title card, an author card, and a subject card.

- The call number helps you find the book on the shelves.

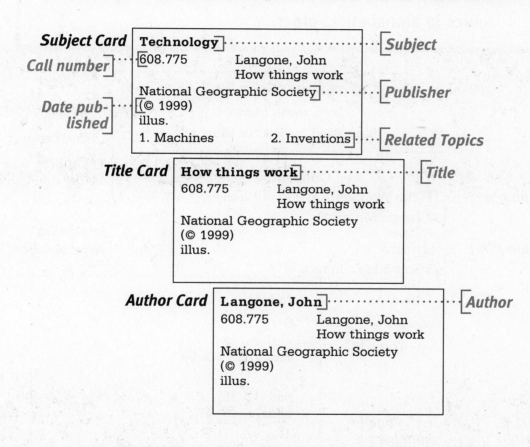

Subject Card
Call number
Date published

Technology · **Subject**
608.775   Langone, John
             How things work
National Geographic Society · · · · · · · · **Publisher**
(© 1999)
illus.
1. Machines   2. Inventions · · · **Related Topics**

Title Card

How things work · · · · · · · · · · · · · · · · · · **Title**
608.775   Langone, John
             How things work
National Geographic Society
(© 1999)
illus.

Author Card

Langone, John · · · · · · · · · · · · · · · · · · · **Author**
608.775   Langone, John
             How things work
National Geographic Society
(© 1999)
illus.

Practice Use the cards above to answer these questions.

1. What is the title of John Langone's book?

2. What is the call number of this book?

3. If you wanted to find a book about machines, which type of card would you use?

4. If you knew the author's name but not the title, which type of card would you use?

5. If you knew the book's title, which type of card would you use?

Build Skills

Parts of a Book

DEFINITIONS

- The title page of a book tells the title of the book, the author's name, and the illustrator's name.

- The table of contents lists the titles and beginning page numbers of all the chapters or parts of the book.

- The index at the back of a book lists all the important topics in alphabetical order.

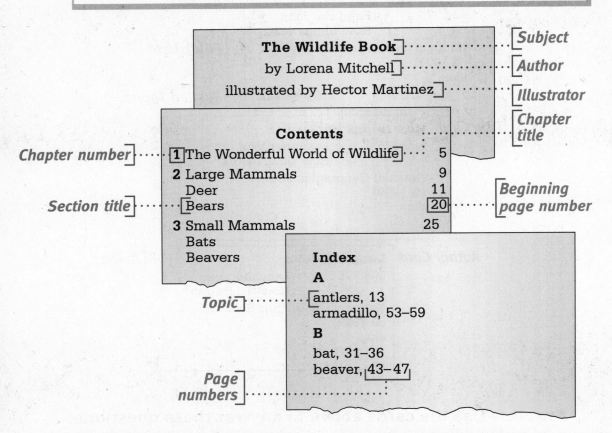

Practice Use the title page, table of contents, and index above to answer the following questions.

1. Who is the author of *The Wildlife Book*?

2. What is the title of Chapter 2 of the book?

3. On what page does the subtopic titled "Bears" begin?

4. On what pages can you find information about armadillos?

5. On what pages would you find information about beavers?

Note-taking and Summarizing

Build Skills

DEFINITIONS

- When you read articles for information, you can take notes on the main idea and the important details.

- You can use your notes to write a summary. A summary tells in a few sentences the main idea and the important details.

Zebras

Zebras are members of the horse family. They look like horses, but they have white and black or dark brown stripes. No zebra has exactly the same stripes as another.

A zebra's stripes help confuse its enemies. A hungry lion may see the stripes, not the zebra.

Notes

part of horse family
stripes—white and black or dark brown
no stripes the same
zebra's stripes protect it

Summary

Zebras belong to the horse family. The zebras' stripes help hide them from their enemies. All zebras have stripes. No two patterns are the same.

Practice Read the article, the notes, and the summary. Then answer the following questions.

1. What is the article about?

2. What is the main idea of the last paragraph?

3. To what family do zebras belong?

4. What color are a zebra's stripes?

5. Why is the summary shorter than the article?

Build Skills

Library Catalog Menu

> ### DEFINITIONS
>
> - In most libraries, the catalog, or PAC (Public Access Catalog), is on the computer.
>
> - All books are listed by author, title, and subject.
>
> - Click on the menu to start your search.
>
> - Type in the key words, names, or titles in the search field.

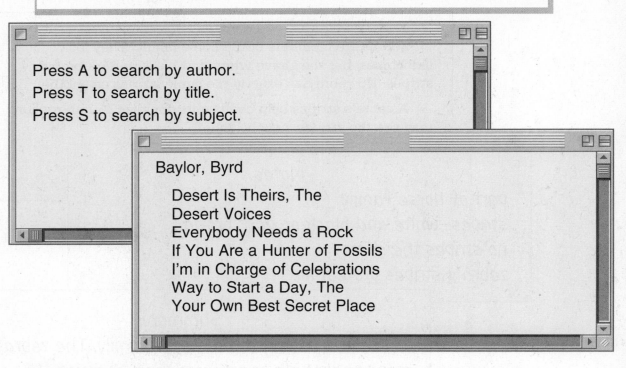

Press A to search by author.
Press T to search by title.
Press S to search by subject.

Baylor, Byrd

Desert Is Theirs, The
Desert Voices
Everybody Needs a Rock
If You Are a Hunter of Fossils
I'm in Charge of Celebrations
Way to Start a Day, The
Your Own Best Secret Place

Practice Use the computer screens above to answer the following questions.

1. If you were looking for books on a specific subject, how would you start your search?

2. What would you type in the search field to find books by an author whose name you know?

3. If you knew the title of the book, but not the author's name, how would you start your search?

4. If you wanted to find a book titled *The Cloud Book,* how would you start your search?

5. How did the person find a list of books by Byrd Baylor?

Periodicals

DEFINITIONS

- Magazines and newspapers are called periodicals. They are good sources for up-to-date information.

- Magazines often cover many topics. Some magazines are about a single topic. Magazines may be published once a week or once a month.

- Newspapers contain local, state, national, and world current events. Most newspapers are published every day.

- Your library may have a guide to periodicals that will lead you to newspaper or magazine articles on a topic.

Practice Look at the newspaper and magazine covers. Think about the kind of information you could find in each. Then write the name of the one that you might use to find the following stories or information.

1. the score of yesterday's baseball game in Middletown

2. an article about camping equipment

3. "Basketball Stars of Tomorrow"

4. "How to Build a Bookcase"

5. "Tango—the New Dance Craze"

Build Skills

Build Skills

Graphs

DEFINITIONS

- A graph is a diagram that shows the relationship between two or more things. You can use a graph to compare information.

- A line graph shows changes or differences over a period of time. It uses lines to join points that stand for numbers.

- A bar graph compares facts. It uses bars that go across or up and down.

- A circle graph compares parts of a whole. You can compare the sizes of the parts into which the circle is divided.

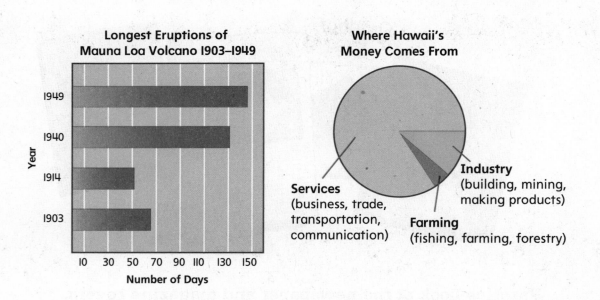

Longest Eruptions of Mauna Loa Volcano 1903–1949

Where Hawaii's Money Comes From

Services (business, trade, transportation, communication)

Industry (building, mining, making products)

Farming (fishing, farming, forestry)

Practice Use the graphs above to answer the questions.

1. How many years does the bar graph show?

2. When was the longest eruption of Mauna Loa?

3. Was there a longer eruption in 1914 or in 1903?

4. According to the circle graph, what are the three ways that Hawaii makes money?

5. Where does most of Hawaii's money come from?

Internet: Online Search

DEFINITIONS

- **The Internet** is a system that lets computers all over the world talk to each other. It can help you research a topic.

- A **search engine** is a tool that searches the Internet for Web sites on your topic.

- A **Web site** is a page or series of pages with information on a topic. To find a Web site on your topic, do a **key word search** by typing in a subject.

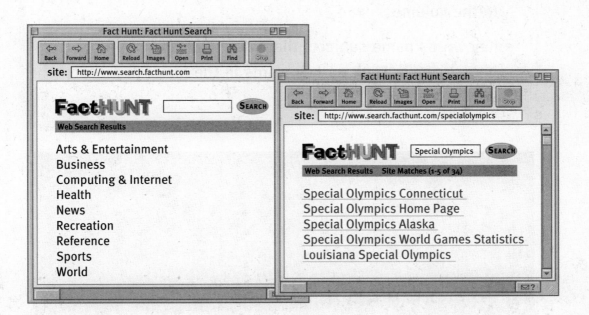

Practice Use the computer screens above to answer the following questions.

1. Which search engine was chosen?

2. What is the topic of the search?

3. How many Web sites did the search find?

4. What Web address might you click on to find out more about the Special Olympics in Alaska?

5. Which Web site might have more general information about the Special Olympics?

Build Skills

Encyclopedia

DEFINITIONS

- An encyclopedia contains articles about people, places, things, and events.

- Articles in an encyclopedia often answer these questions: *Who? What? Where? When? Why? How?*

- The articles are arranged in alphabetical order in books called *volumes*.

- Each volume is labeled with a number and one or more letters that stand for the beginning letters of the subjects in the volume.

- Key words name subjects that you might find in an encyclopedia. Look up key words in the *index* to research your subject.

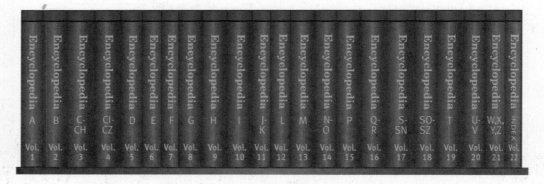

Practice Write the key word or words that you would look up in an encyclopedia to find information about each subject. Then write the letter or letters of the volume in which you would find each key word.

1. George Washington's birthplace

2. an elephant's trunk

3. holidays in Japan

4. important dates in California history

5. how volcanoes are formed

Telephone Directory

DEFINITIONS

- The telephone directory is a list of names, addresses, and telephone numbers.

- The White Pages list the names of people and companies in ABC order.

- The Yellow Pages list the names of different types of businesses. Within each group, businesses are listed in ABC order.

- Emergency numbers for police, ambulance, and fire department are found at the front of the telephone directory.

- Guide words at the top of each page give the first and last names on the page.

HEALTH CLUBS

Family Fitness Center
   197 Federal St., Greenfield 555-1023
Karate for Kids
   40 Bank Row, Conway 555-4139

▶ **Hospitals**

County Hospital
   8 Valley View Dr., Conway 555-3295
West Medical Center
   35 Lee Rd., Greenfield 555-5775

Dorman—Dumont

Dorman, Eric 47 Gothic St., Amherst. . . 555-9521
Dougherty, Kay & David
   148 Wells St., Greenfield. 555-3384
Dove's Nest Restaurant
   35 Amberton Rd., Sunderland. 555-7168
Downey, Henry T 3 Elm Terr., Conway. . 555-8050
Dumont Country Store
   221 Hendrick Ave., E. Hampton. 555-6579

Practice Use the telephone directory pages above to answer the following questions.

1. What is Eric Dorman's telephone number?

2. What is the address of Karate for Kids?

3. What number would you call for the Family Fitness Center?

4. What is Henry Downey's address?

5. What number would you call for the County Hospital?

Build Skills

Thesaurus

DEFINITIONS

- A **thesaurus** is a book that gives synonyms for many common words. **Synonyms** are words that have the same or almost the same meaning.

- The words in a thesaurus are listed in **alphabetical order**.

- Under each **entry word** is a list of synonyms, their definitions, and a sample sentence.

- Some entries also have **antonyms**, words with opposite meanings.

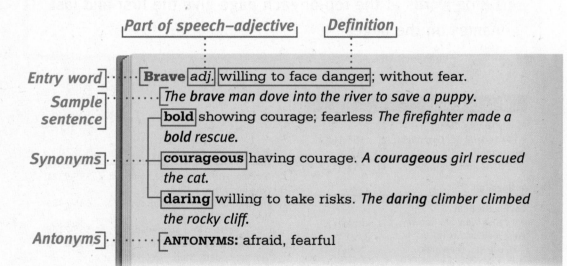

Practice Use the thesaurus entries above to answer the following questions.

1. What are the synonyms for *brave*?

2. Which synonym means "willing to take risks"?

3. What synonym would you use to describe someone who acts without fear?

4. What is the definition of *courageous*?

5. What antonyms are given for the word *brave*?

Map/Atlas

Build Skills

DEFINITIONS

- A **map** is a drawing that shows all or part of Earth's surface.

- The **compass rose** on a map shows direction.

- A map has pictures on it called **symbols**. The **key** explains the meaning of the symbols.

- The **scale bar** shows how distances on the map relate to distances in the real world.

- An **atlas** is a book of maps.

- The **index** of an atlas shows the page numbers of all the maps in the atlas.

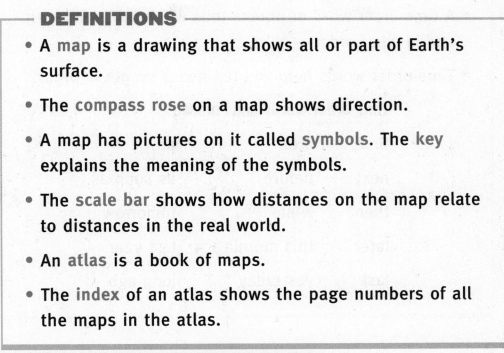

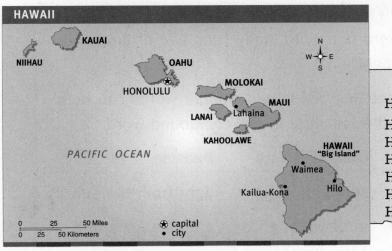

INDEX

Havasu, Lake, Ariz. 211 J2

Havasupai IR, Ariz. 211 D7

Haverhill, Mass. 41 B9

Hawaii 281

Hawaii (Island), Hawaii 281 K25

Hays, Kans. 179 D8

Haystack Mountain, Vt. 53 T4

Practice Use the map and index above to answer the following questions.

1. What is the capital of Hawaii?

2. In what direction from Maui is Lanai, east or west?

3. What are the names of two cities on the island of Hawaii (the Big Island)?

4. Is the island of Lanai north or south of Molokai?

5. On what page of this atlas can you find the map of Hawaii?

Build Skills

RULE 1

Time-Order Words

- A time-order word or phrase tells when things happen and in what order.

- Time-order words help you tell about events in order.

Time-Order Words and Phrases

first	after	now
next	before	as soon as
then	while	tomorrow
later	this morning	last year
last	yesterday	long ago

RULE 2

Compound Words

- A compound word is a word made from two or more words joined together.

- Knowing the meaning of the two smaller words can help you figure out the meaning of the compound word.

Two Words	Compound Word	Meaning
sun + light	sunlight	light from the sun
bird + house	birdhouse	a house for a bird
sea + shell	seashell	a shell from the sea
paint + brush	paintbrush	a brush for paint
hand + made	handmade	made by hand
note + book	notebook	a book for notes
bath + tub	bathtub	a tub for a bath
snow + ball	snowball	a ball made of snow
sail + boat	sailboat	a boat with a sail

Build Skills

RULE 3 — **Prefixes**

- A prefix is a word part that is added to the beginning of a word.

- A prefix changes the meaning of a word.

Prefix	Meaning	Example
un-	not, the opposite of	*untie*
re-	again, back	*rebuild*
dis-	not, the opposite of	*disappear*
pre-	before	*preschool*

RULE 4 — **Suffixes**

- A suffix is a word part that is added to the end of a base word.

- A suffix changes the meaning of the base word.

Suffix	Meaning	Example
-er	person who	*manager*
-or	person who	*spectator*
-less	without	*careless*
-able	able to be	*readable*
-ly	in a certain way	*suddenly*
-ful	full of	*hopeful*

Build Skills

RULE 5

Homophones

- Words that sound alike but have different spellings and different meanings are called homophones.

- You must use context to figure out which spelling of a homophone is correct.

Homophones

hi	high
be	bee
sun	son
eye	I
blue	blew
hole	whole
rode	road, rowed
to	two, too
nose	knows
horse	hoarse
see	sea
flour	flower
would	wood
right	write
there	their

Build Skills

RULE 6

Synonyms and Antonyms

- **Synonyms** are words that have the same or almost the same meaning.

- **Antonyms** are words that have opposite meanings.

Word	Synonym	Antonym
big	large	small
cold	icy	warm
strong	firm	weak
glad	happy	unhappy
fast	quick	slow
below	under	above
dark	dim	bright
friend	pal	enemy
let	allow	deny
ask	question	answer
like	love	dislike
laugh	giggle	cry

Build Skills

Problem Words

The English language includes some confusing words that are often used incorrectly. The following charts will help you understand how to use these words in the correct way.

Words	Correct Usage	Correct Usage
bad/badly	*Bad* is an adjective used to describe a noun. It means "the opposite of good." *That fruit left a bad taste in my mouth.*	*Badly* is an adverb that tells "how" about a verb. It means "in a bad way." *He tied the knot badly because he rushed.*
beside/besides	*Beside* means "next to." *Kim sat beside me at the play.*	*Besides* means "in addition to." *Besides art and math, she likes music best.*
can/may	*Can* means "be able to." *Most foxes can run very fast.*	*May* means "be permitted to." *Each student may borrow three books.*
good/well	*Good* is an adjective used to describe a noun. *We had a good time at the zoo.*	*Well* is usually an adverb. It describes a verb by telling "how." *Sara's soccer team played well and won.*
in/into	*In* means "inside." *Are your books in your book bag?*	*Into* means "moving to the inside of." *I put the quarter into my piggy bank.*
its/it's	*Its* is a possessive pronoun. *Its* does not have an apostrophe. *The dog wagged its tail.*	*It's* is a contraction for "it is." The apostrophe takes the place of the *i* in *is*. *It's a cold, rainy day.*

Build Skills

Words	Correct Usage	Correct Usage
lay/lie	*Lay* means "to put something down." *Lay the books gently on the table.*	*Lie* means "to rest on something." *My cat likes to lie on a soft pillow.*
loose/lose	*Loose* means "not tight." *My little sister has a loose tooth.*	*Lose* means "to be missing something." *Did Sam lose his notebook?*
set/sit	*Set* means "to put in a certain place." *Mom set the dish on the counter.*	*Sit* means "to be seated." *Let's sit here and watch the game.*
than/then	*Than* means "compared to." *My brother's bike is newer than mine.*	*Then* means "after that." *Ali did her homework and then played outside.*
their/they're	*Their* is a possessive pronoun that means "belonging to them." *Lee and Lin showed us their shell collection.*	*They're* is a contraction for "they are." *They're ready to sing the new song.*
your/you're	*Your* is a possessive pronoun that means "belonging to you." *Is your birthday this month?*	*You're* is a contraction for "you are." *You're so funny when you tell a joke.*

QUICK WRITE Create your own chart of problem words. Include words from this chart or other words you sometimes get confused. Write sentences to help you remember how to use the words correctly.

Build Skills

Easily Confused Words

Some words are easily confused because they are spelled in a similar way or because they sound alike. These words have different meanings, so you need to be sure you use the correct one.

all ready	breath	desert	hour	picture	tired
already	breathe	dessert	our	pitcher	tried
an	close	ever	lay	quiet	wander
and	clothes	every	lie	quite	wonder
any more	cloth	farther	loose	share	weather
anymore	clothe	further	lose	sure	whether
any way	costume	for	marry	than	were
anyway	custom	four	merry	then	where
bean	dairy	hear	of	though	your
been	diary	here	off	through	you're

Frequently Misspelled Words

For many writers, some words are hard to spell. You can use this list to check your spelling.

a lot	brother	enough	I'm	often	they
again	brought	every	instead	once	thought
against	busy	family	let's	outside	together
all right	buy	favorite	library	people	tomorrow
already	caught	finally	listen	probably	trouble
always	certain	first	live	really	upon
answer	charge	found	love	receive	we'll
around	country	friend	many	rhyme	we're
balloon	cousin	guess	might	said	when
because	different	half	minute	school	while
before	does	happened	neighbor	since	won't
believe	dollar	have	ninety	straight	word
bicycle	done	heard	nothing	surprise	work

Build Skills

Common Homophones

Homophones are words that sound the same but are spelled differently and have different meanings. *Blew* and *blue* are examples of homophones.

ad	dear	I	one	sail	wait
add	deer	eye	won	sale	weight
ate	fair	its	pail	son	way
eight	fare	it's	pale	sun	weigh
bare	flour	knew	peace	tail	weak
bear	flower	new	piece	tale	week
beat	for	know	plain	their	wear
beet	four	no	plane	there	where
blew	hear	knows	right	they're	who's
blue	here	nose	write	threw	whose
buy	heard	made	road	through	wood
by	herd	maid	rode	to	would
cent	hole	meat		too	your
sent	whole	meet		two	you're

Build Skills

Spelling Rules and Strategies

1. When words end in silent *e,* drop the *e* when adding an ending that begins with a vowel. *(like + ed = liked)* When adding an ending that begins with a consonant, keep the silent *e.* *(nice + ly = nicely)*

2. When a base word ends with a consonant followed by *y,* change the *y* to *i* when adding any ending except endings that begin with *i.* *(try + es = tries; try + ing = trying)*

3. When a base word ends with a vowel followed by *y,* do not change the *y* when adding suffixes or endings. *(key + s = keys)*

4. When a one-syllable word ends in one vowel followed by one consonant, double the consonant before adding an ending that begins with a vowel. *(stop + ing = stopping)*

5. The letter *q* is always followed by *u. (quick, quite)*

6. No English words end in *j, q,* or *v.*

7. Add *-s* to most words to form plurals or present-tense verbs. Add *-es* to words ending in *x, z, s, sh,* or *ch.* *(fork + s = forks; dish + es = dishes; glass + es = glasses)*

8. To make plurals of words that end with one *f* or *fe,* you often need to change the *f* or *fe* to *v* and add *-es.* *(wolf + es = wolves)*

9. When the /s/ sound is spelled *c, c* is always followed by *e, i,* or *y. (trace, city, bicycle)*

10. When /j/ is spelled *g, g* is always followed by *e, i,* or *y.* *(gentle, giant, gym)*

11. Short vowels are followed by *dge.* Long vowels are followed by *ge. (edge, cage)*

12. If the /ch/ sound immediately follows a short vowel in a one-syllable word, it is spelled *tch.* There are a few exceptions in English: *much, such, which,* and *rich.*

Build Skills

Use these strategies to help you become a better speller.

1. Learn common homophones and make sure you have used the correct homophone in your writing.
They ate ***their*** lunch. They sat over ***there.***
It's a pretty cat. ***Its*** name is Bell.

2. Think of a word you know, such as a rhyming word, that has the same spelling pattern as the word you want to spell. (***play, day, gray***)

3. Use words that you know how to spell to help you spell new words: (***gl***ad + sn***ow*** = ***glow***)

4. Make up clues to help you remember the spelling. (***u*** and ***i b***u***ild a house; a p***i***ece of p***i***e; the princip***al*** is your p***al***)

5. Think of a related word to help you spell a word with a silent letter or a hard-to-hear sound. (***sign–signal; rel***a***tive–rel***a***ted***)

6. Divide the word into syllables. (***mul ti ply***)

7. Learn to spell prefixes and suffixes you use often in writing.

8. Look for word chunks or smaller words that help you remember the spelling of the word.
(***hippopotamus = hippo pot am us***)

9. Change the way you say the word to yourself to help with the spelling. (***knife = /ke nif/; beauty = /be e u te/***)

10. Think of times you may have seen the word in reading, on signs, or in a textbook. Try to remember how it looked. Write the word in different ways. Which one looks correct? (***adress, addres, address***)

11. Keep an alphabetical Personal Word List in your Spelling Journal. Write words you often have trouble spelling.

12. Become familiar with the dictionary and use it often.

Correcting Sentence Fragments

- A **sentence** is a group of words that expresses a complete thought.

- A **sentence fragment** is a group of words that does not express a complete thought.

Problem 1

A sentence fragment that does not have a subject

Sentence Fragment: *Came for Greg today.*

> Who or what came for Greg today?

Solution 1

Who or **what** is the **subject** of the sentence? You must add a subject to each sentence fragment to make it a complete sentence.

Sentence: *A letter came for Greg today.*

Problem 2

A sentence fragment that does not have a predicate

Sentence Fragment: *Greg's family.*

> What about Greg's family?

Solution 2

The part of a sentence that tells what the subject does or is is called the **predicate**. You must add a predicate to the sentence fragment to make it a complete sentence.

Sentence: *Greg's family invited Carlos for a visit.*

Problem 3

A fragment that does not have either a subject or a predicate

Sentence Fragment: *From Argentina.*

Who is this about?
Who is from
Argentina?

Solution 3

A complete sentence must tell who or what. It must tell what the subject does or is. You must add a subject and a verb to make the sentence fragment a complete sentence.

Sentence: *Carlos is from Argentina.*

Practice Rewrite the sentence fragments correctly. Add a subject, a predicate, or a subject and a predicate.

1. Carlos speaks Spanish. Is the main language of Argentina.

2. Carlos also speaks English. He and his friends.

3. Greg speaks a little Spanish. Many new words from Carlos.

4. Carlos and his friends play soccer. Play soccer, too.

5. Greg writes back to Carlos. All about his last game.

Correcting Run-on Sentences

- A **sentence** is a group of words that expresses a complete thought.

- A **run-on sentence** joins together two or more sentences that should be written separately.

Problem 1

Two sentences joined with no punctuation between them

> **Run-on Sentence:** *Cats make great pets they are funny and lovable.*

> *What are the two ideas in the run-on sentence?*

Solution 1

You can correct a run-on sentence by separating two complete ideas into **two sentences**.

> **Two Sentences:** *Cats make great pets. They are funny and lovable.*

Problem 2

Two sentences joined with only a comma

> **Run-on Sentence:** *I held the cat in my lap, he slept all the way home.*

> *Where should the word and go to join the two ideas?*

Solution 2

Add *and* to correct the sentences. You also need to use a **comma** before *and* to join them.

> **Compound Sentence:** *I held the cat in my lap, and he slept all the way home.*

Problem 3

Three or more sentences joined with *and*

Run-on Sentence: *Our cat fetches like a dog and he pounces on paper and pretzels are his favorite snack.*

> What are the three ideas in this run-on sentence?

Solution 3

When three or more sentences are joined by *and*, you need to break them into shorter sentences.

Shorter Sentences: *Our cat fetches like a dog. He pounces on paper. Pretzels are his favorite snack.*

Practice Rewrite each run-on sentence correctly.

1. I have a new book about cats Mom bought it yesterday.

2. I read some of the book last night, it is really interesting.

3. The book has many helpful hints and it tells the history of cats and it gives amazing facts.

4. A cat named Ma lived 34 years, a tabby cat named Joseph weighed 48 pounds.

5. I will finish the book soon then you can borrow it.

Confusing Plurals and Possessives

- A **plural noun** names more than one person, place, or thing.

- A **possessive noun** is a noun that shows who or what owns or has something.

Problem 1

Using an apostrophe in a plural noun

Incorrect: *My friend's spot a nest in a tree.*

> Does a spot belong to one friend?

Solution 1

Take out the apostrophe to correct a plural noun.

Correct: *My friends spot a nest in a tree.*

Problem 2

Leaving out the apostrophe in a possessive noun

Incorrect: *A hornets nest is made from chewed-up wood.*

> Does one or more than one have something?

Solution 2

A **singular possessive noun** shows what one person, place, or thing has. You need to add an apostrophe (') and an *-s* to a singular noun to make it possessive.

Correct: *A hornet's nest is made from chewed-up wood.*

Problem 3

Putting the apostrophe in the wrong place in a plural possessive noun

Incorrect: *Hornets are gardener's friends.*

> Ask yourself: "Does the plural of *gardener* add *s*?"

Solution 3

Add an apostrophe to make most plural nouns possessive.

Correct: *Hornets are gardeners' friends.*

Practice **Rewrite the sentences. Write any incorrect plural nouns and possessive nouns correctly.**

1. Hornets are related to yellow jackets. Both insects' build nests the same way.

2. Yellow jackets sometimes build in gophers' holes. Empty field mices' holes are good, too.

3. Hornets' markings are yellow or white. Yellow jackets stripes are yellow and black.

4. Al's book has many photographs. The books title is *Bees, Wasps, and Other Insects.*

5. The photographers' names are Jason and Ann Lee. What is the authors name?

Lack of Subject-Verb Agreement

- A verb in the present tense must agree with its subject.

- Do not add -*s* or -*es* to a present-tense verb when the subject is plural.

Problem 1

Using a plural verb with a singular subject

No Agreement: *Mom look over her plans for a garden.*

> *Is Mom a singular subject or a plural subject?*

Solution 1

When the subject of a sentence is one person or thing, the verb must tell about one person or thing. Add -*s* or -*es* to a present-tense verb to make the subject and verb agree.

Agreement: *Mom looks over her plans for a garden.*

Problem 2

Using a singular verb with plural subject or *I* or *you*

No Agreement: *My sisters goes to the garden center for seeds.*

> *How can the verb agree with its subject?*

Solution 2

When the subject of a sentence is more than one person or thing or *I* or *you*, you do not need to add -*s* or -*es* to a present-tense verb.

Agreement: *My sisters go to the garden center for seeds.*

Using a singular verb when a subject has two or more nouns joined by *and*

No Agreement: *Lisa and my little sister plants the seeds.*

> How many nouns are in the subject?

Solution 3

When the subject of a sentence has two nouns joined by *and*, you do not add *-s* or *-es* to a present-tense verb. Take out *-s* or *-es* to make the subject and verb agree.

Agreement: *Lisa and my little sister plant the seeds.*

Practice Rewrite the sentences correctly. Make the subject and verb in each sentence agree.

1. Everyone cleans up. Even Fuzzer help.

2. Lisa and Ellie put away the hand tools. Dad and Mom rewinds the hose.

3. I put away the shovel. Then you empties the wheelbarrow.

4. Two weeks pass by. Tiny plants finally pops up through the soil.

5. My family and I water and weed the garden. Before long Lisa, Ellie, and I picks vegetables.

Troubleshooter

Incorrect Verb Forms

- An **irregular verb** has a special spelling to show the past tense.

- Some irregular verbs have a special spelling when used with the helping verb *have*.

Problem 1

Forming the past tense of an irregular verb incorrectly

Incorrect: *My friend Anna comed to New York with us.*

> Is come an irregular verb?

Solution 1

Some verbs are **irregular**. You do not add *-ed* to show actions in the past. Use the special forms of the irregular verbs.

Correct: *My friend Anna came to New York with us.*

Problem 2

Using incorrect irregular verb form for past tense

Incorrect: *We seen many interesting sights.*

> Which sounds right: "We seen" or "We saw"?

Solution 2

For irregular verbs, you do not add *-ed* to show actions in the past. You need to use the special forms of the irregular verbs.

Correct: *We saw many interesting sights.*

Problem 3

Using incorrect irregular verb form for past with *have*

Incorrect: *I have never saw the Statue of Liberty before.*

Should *have, has,* or *had* go with *saw* or *seen?*

Solution 3

The helping verb *have* helps the main verb tell about an action. You know that some irregular verbs change their spelling in the past tense and when they are used with the helping verb *have*. Change the verb form to the one used with *have*.

Correct: *I have never seen the Statue of Liberty before.*

Practice **Rewrite the sentences. Use the correct verb forms.**

1. Our class had to do oral reports. I done mine on our trip to New York.

2. I finished my scrapbook just in time. I bringed it to school.

3. Rita asked about the Statue of Liberty. Mike said he seen it last summer.

4. Have you been to New York City? Have you saw the Statue of Liberty?

5. Everyone liked my report. I sayed, "I'm glad."

Incorrect Use of Pronouns

- A **pronoun** must match the noun or nouns that it refers to.
- A **subject pronoun** is used as the subject of a sentence.
- An **object pronoun** is part of the predicate.
- Do not confuse **possessive pronouns** with contractions.

Problem 1

Using object pronouns as subjects

Incorrect: *Her and I enjoyed playing the piano.*

> How does the sentence sound without *and I*?

Solution 1

Replace the object pronoun with a **subject pronoun**. Subject pronouns include *I, you, he, she, it, we,* and *they*.

Correct: *She and I enjoyed playing the piano.*

Problem 2

Using subject pronouns in the predicate

Incorrect: *Scales are easier for me than for she.*

> Is *she* used as the subject or as the object?

Solution 2

Replace the subject pronoun with an **object pronoun**. Object pronouns include *me, you, him, her, it, us,* and *them*.

Correct: *Scales are easier for me than for her.*

254

Problem 3

Confusing contractions and possessive pronouns

Incorrect: *You're mother's lesson is on Monday.*

> Can you say "You are" instead of "You're"?

Solution 3

A possessive pronoun shows who or what owns something. A pronoun-verb contraction is a shortened form of a pronoun and a verb. It has an apostrophe.

Correct: *Your mother's lesson is on Monday.*

Practice **Rewrite the sentences. Write the pronouns, contractions, and possessive pronouns correctly.**

1. We have our first recital soon. Mom and me are nervous.

2. Mrs. Lowski said, "You're ready." She added, "So is you're mother."

3. I played my piece for Dad and my sister. Him and her really liked it.

4. Then Mom played for Dad, Patty, and me. She made they and me proud.

5. My friends say they're coming. Their proud of me.

Incorrect Use of Adjectives

- You can use **adjectives** to compare two or more nouns.
- Add *-er* to an adjective to compare two nouns.
- Add *-est* to compare more than two nouns.

Problem 1

Forming adjectives that compare incorrectly

Incorrect: *Is the Nile River the longer river in the world?*

> Are you comparing two or more than two?

Solution 1

Count how many people, places, or things you are comparing. Then add *-er* or *-est*.

Correct: *Is the Nile River the longest river in the world?*

Practice Rewrite each sentence. Write the adjectives that compare correctly.

1. Is the Rocky Mountain range longest than the Appalachian Mountain range?

2. Is Asia, North America, or Africa the world's greater continent of all?

3. Is the Pacific Ocean deepest than the Atlantic Ocean?

4. Is the Atacama Desert in Chile the drier place on Earth?

5. Where is the world's older capital city of all?